BEGINNING

Part One

Peacemaking T

BEGINNING NOW

Part One

Peacemaking Theology

A study book
for individuals and groups

Rowan Williams & Mark Collier

DUNAMIS
St James's · London
1984

Published by Dunamis at St James's
197 Piccadilly, London W1V 9LF

Phototypeset by Getset (BTS) Ltd, Eynsham, Oxford
and printed in Great Britain at the Alden Press, Oxford

British Library Cataloguing in Publication Data
Beginning now.
Pt.1: Peacemaking theology.
1. Church of England 2. Church group work 3. Peace—Religious aspects—Church of England
I. Williams, Rowan II. Collier, Mark
261.8′73 BV652.2

ISBN 0 947546 00 6

Contents

Foreword

This book, along with its companion volume, is the result of an initiative taken by Dunamis in 1983.

DUNAMIS is a church-based educational foundation which was formed in 1980 to explore issues of personal, national and international security in the modern age. The name derives from the Greek word for power.

Dunamis is based at St James's Church, Piccadilly, but is open to those of any religious belief or none. It has no dogmatic commitment to any particular solution for the problems of security in the nuclear age, but is committed to:

1. creating a forum to explore both traditional and alternative approaches to the pursuit of international security;
2. examining the profound psychological, moral and spiritual links between personal security and the security of nations;
3. holding up a vision of a more stable and just world order than that represented by two adversary blocs, and so playing a part in building bridges between the world's Rich North and Poor South — the latter being the human majority.

Dunamis is currently active in the following areas:

1. Public lectures and discussions at St James's Church, Piccadilly

Dunamis takes full advantage of the drawing power of St James's to attract a series of very high-calibre speakers of widely differing views.

2. Educational materials

Dunamis records all these talks and sells them as educational tapes; it also sells a range of books on issues of international security from both Christian and secular viewpoints. From time to time Dunamis publishes its own materials, such as the present book.

3. Private seminars

Following some of the public lectures, Dunamis invites people in positions of authority, influence or leadership to a small private supper to discuss the issues raised by the lecturer. Members of Parliament of all parties, civil servants, academics, journalists, clergy and people from industry and commerce are regularly invited. These groups have frequently been joined by diplomats, including British, European, American, Soviet and Chinese.

4. Dunamis groups

Dunamis has been helping churches of all denominations in various parts of the country to set up groups to study the necessary connection between their moral, religious and personal beliefs, and the problems of contemporary international life.

5. North/South

The Brandt Report has made it clear that the fundamental questions of social and economic justice have been grossly neglected and that these, too, have vital connections with the prospects for international order. Dunamis is making its own contribution to bridging this gap by working in partnership with a group of co-operative farms in Zimbabwe, to provide training programmes in farm management, financial control and appropriate technology. This is known as the Jangano Project, Jangano being a Shona word meaning 'working together'.

6. Working parties

The Dunamis initiative in 1983 to set up ecumenical working parties on the 'Theology of Peacemaking' has been supported by the Archbishop of Canterbury, Cardinal Hume, and Kenneth Greet, former moderator of the Free Church Federal Council.

These working parties met during 1983 and produced valuable papers on aspects of peace, justice, security and related issues. From these papers, Dunamis staff were able to gauge something of the current thinking on these issues in the churches. It was intended from the start that the fruits of these working parties would result in materials which would enable Christians of all denominations to further their understanding of the biblical roots of the call to peacemaking.

The two volumes of *Beginning Now* have sought to remain faithful to the issues and concerns raised by members of the working parties. The authors have endeavoured to provide material that will advance Christian understanding of peacemaking in theory and in practice, without being partisan or advocating any particular programme or set of policies for peacemaking.

The authors wish to express their thanks to the members of the working parties for all their hard work. As authors, of course, they accept final responsibility for the contents of their respective books: these do not necessarily express the views of Dunamis, which takes up no single or corporate position.

Introduction

This book, Part 1 of *Beginning Now*, seeks to show how ideas of peace and peacemaking are central to the scriptural tradition. We have not attempted to say everything that could be said on the matter, nor to have the last word on 'peace' — after all, this book is called *Beginning* Now! What we have tried to provide is a study book, which does not presuppose a great deal of background knowledge, explaining why we think it is important for Christians to see themselves as peacemakers in the world.

We have chosen to focus this book on the study of biblical themes, because the Bible provides a common root and starting point for Christians of all denominations and political persuasions. This does not mean that we think it is possible to make simple comparisons between situations in the Bible and our present-day concerns — the Bible is not an instruction manual that will solve all our problems that easily! However, there are *parallels* between the great human and social dilemmas that we face today and some of the issues that the biblical writers were concerned with. If we believe that the biblical tradition reveals God's action in the world, then in turning to the Bible we can hope to discover some clues about what it is that God requires of us. To translate God's commands into the everyday realities of social and political life is a task requiring lifelong commitment in faith to prayer, study and action.

In this book, we trace some of the great issues and dilemmas (security, integrity, identity, power, conflict, enemies) in certain biblical stories. We look at the biblical words for peace — *shalom* and *eirene* — and try to understand what those words meant to the writers who used them. We look at what it means that we should love and trust God, both as individuals and as the community of the Church, and so at the way in which our peacemaking and our praying are inseparably linked.

Figure 1 is a summary of the main themes of this book, showing how they fit together and follow on from each other.

In each section we invite you to relate the biblical material to contemporary issues.

How to use this book

As the title indicates, we intend this book either for individual study or as the basis for group discussion. In either case, one way of using the book is to study

Chapter 1 → Israel had a dilemma about its *security* as a nation: how to be secure against enemies while still preserving its integrity and identity as the People of God. Its solution was two-fold:

Work for peace, both within the community and without

Love and trust God

Chapter 2 → What is the meaning of *peace*? In the Bible, the words for peace are *shalom* (in the OT) and *eirene* (in the NT). For the biblical writers, 'peace' is inseparable from justice

Chapter 3 → Israel as a *community* of faith had to learn what trust in God meant. It did not mean safety, or easy comfort. Rather, Israel had to be ready to take risks in order to remain faithful to the covenant. The Christian Church, as the new covenant community, must also be willing to take risks if it is to be faithful to God's call to make peace

Chapter 4 → As *individuals* we must learn to love and trust God. We can only learn this through prayer, which will also prepare us to be peacemakers in the world.

Chapter 5 → As we seek to make peace, both within the community of the Church, and in the world at large, we will have to come to terms with those who have *power*, and we will find ourselves in the midst of *conflict*. The reconciliation of the Gospel is to create peace with justice

Chapter 6 → In order to create *shalom* we have to confront our *enemies*. We must let go of personal and social needs for enemies, and obey Jesus' call to love those who oppose us

Beginning Now, Part 2 → In order to respond to the scriptural call to create *shalom* in the world, we must not only study and pray, but also be active in practical ways. Our everyday lives are full of opportunities for *peacemaking in practice*

Figure 1. Summary of the main themes of this book.

the chapters in the order they are written, using Figure 1 as a guide to the relationships between the chapters. At various points in the writing there are examples and questions for discussion.

If you are a member of a group meeting to study this book, it is a good idea if everyone reads a given chapter, or portion of a chapter, before the meeting. It will also help to have read the biblical passages referred to in that chapter. If this preparation is done, each person can come to the group knowing which points they are particularly interested in, what they want to discuss, and maybe having already thought a little about the questions given.

If you are studying this book alone, the 'questions for discussion' will give you food for thought, and may help you in deciding how relevant the biblical material is to your concerns.

Rather than reading all the chapters in order, you may prefer to follow particular themes through the book (*all* the themes stem from the concerns raised in Chapter 1). For instance, if you are interested in the social and political dimensions of peacemaking, then Chapters 1, 2, 5 and 6 form a basis for studying these themes. If you are interested in the more personal dimensions then Chapter 1, the introduction to Chapter 2, followed by Chapters 3, 4 and 6 form a coherent framework. However, it is important to remember that for the biblical writers, and so for us in writing this book, there is no final separation in life and faith between person and society, between private concerns and public issues, between religion and politics, or between peace with God and justice in the world.

We hope that your thoughts and discussions arising from the study of this book will not be restricted to the examples and questions which we give. There are many other issues raised in the course of the book which may well interest you more than the points we have chosen to highlight.

There are further suggestions for discussion and group work on the Group Leaders' Tape: for details, see the order form on the last page of this book.

Beginning now

As we begin this journey and exploration together, as authors and readers, we might recall some words of Jesus:

> He who is not with me is against me (Matt. 12:30)

and

> He who is not against us is on our side. (Mark 9:40)

These two sayings, while similar, have slightly different implications, but, taken together, they say very clearly that there is no neutral ground. We are either with or against what Jesus stood for: we are either creating God's *shalom*, God's reign of peace and justice, or we are destroying it. We have to choose because, as Jesus' words indicate, we cannot be indifferent.

The work of creating *shalom*, of making peace, is part of all the small acts of our daily lives, as well as being part of our larger concerns. The 'coal face', so to speak, is wherever we are.

CHAPTER 1

The dilemma of security

1.1. INTRODUCTION

Consider the following problem: a small kingdom with a distinctive way of life is bordered by neighbouring states that are often unfriendly, in a region overshadowed by a superpower. How can it preserve itself *and its way of life*? Should it throw in its lot with the superpower, by trying to form an alliance on favourable terms? Perhaps. But its bargaining position is not strong—what if the terms are unacceptable? Should it rely on its own military strength to deter aggression, saying, in effect, 'Even if you defeat us it will cost you dear'? Perhaps. But what if the deterrence fails? And even if it succeeds, would it not become a military state, just like its neighbours? What if an emphasis on military values and organisation were *incompatible* with the way of life it was trying to defend? In any case, what is this 'distinctive way of life'—are we talking about its religious practices, the particular form of its government, its economy or what? Indeed, is political independence even *necessary* to preserve that way of life—or would it continue under alien rule, even if, for example, its churches were destroyed and its clergyman enslaved?

The Old Testament deals at length with the problems that just such a country—ancient Israel—had in securing its own identity. Because they had to confront this problem of national security again and again over the centuries, the people of Israel came to recognise that it presented an enduring and insoluble dilemma. That dilemma is what this chapter is all about. Put very simply, the dilemma goes like this: if you try to defend yourself in *this* way, you become vulnerable in *that* way; but if you rely on *that* defence, then you are at risk in *this* way. Or even more starkly: *whatever you do to defend your way of life will soon start to endanger that way of life.*

This is a surprising—and unsettling—lesson to have to learn, and one that the Israelites were understandably reluctant to accept. In order to understand why there was no escaping this conclusion, we will have to begin by sorting out what it was that the Israelites were trying to protect and what it was about their community that they considered essential. So we start by describing briefly the nature and significance of the covenant for the people of Israel and their way of life. The Israelites' special identity and calling as God's chosen people can then provide the background for exploring their problem of national security, and the various ways in which they tried to cope with it. We go on, in Section 1.2, to describe the problems and pitfalls they encountered. This will illustrate in more detail why protecting the integrity—the wholeness and soundness—of the Israelite community posed such an insoluble dilemma.

With this much established, Section 1.3 can consider the lessons that the authors of the Old Testament drew from their experiences. In one sense, the lesson is simple and straightforward: your best hope is to trust in the Lord. But what does that actually mean?—an awful lot of praying? Indeed, is it just the Bible's way of saying 'keep your fingers crossed'? In other words, we start to consider the practical implications of living with the dilemma of security. This continues in the final section where we look at the relevance of Israel's experience for our own times. By this stage it will be clear that, despite all the obvious differences between our time and theirs, the basic dilemma they faced is also our dilemma. So you should be able to decide for yourself which policies and actions concerning defence and national security (either ones that have already been undertaken, or ones that might be undertaken) correspond to the sorts of mistakes and misdirected efforts of the Israelites that you will by then be familiar with. Obviously, just agreeing that this dilemma exists doesn't mean that we can all agree on how precisely we should cope with it. But focusing on the neglected question of just what it is we are trying to defend gives us a more thoughtful basis for starting to consider problems of national security.

In summary then, the aims of this chapter are:

(i) to outline the importance of the covenant for the people of Israel and their way of life;
(ii) to discuss the implications of the covenant for the problem of protecting the Israelite nation when it was threatened by neighbouring states;
(iii) to demonstrate that the basic dilemma faced by the Israelites also poses important questions for our own time.

1.2. ISRAEL'S IDENTITY

Many of the Old Testament scriptures were written, first and foremost, as history books. The authors were trying to record the origins of their society, the development of its institutions and customs, the crises and upheavals it had experienced. But history is seldom written for fun. Usually, historians are trying to make sense of their present-day problems, to understand their own society better, where it has got to and the choices it faces. This is especially so when a society is in a period of rapid change—and, indeed, the same is true of individuals: after some major change in our lives we usually have a different story to tell.

Israel, by the 10th century BC, was in just such a period of social change. There was a great deal more wealth around, and links were developing with other countries, so that regular trade became more important. In the reign of King Solomon, relations with Egypt were particularly strong, and this had one very significant consequence. Egypt was a literate civilisation with a great deal of interest in the forms and techniques of passing on traditions. Around this time, therefore, writers in Israel began to write about the past of their people and to organise their traditions. The changes they were living through gave them the impetus to ask certain questions of their traditions, and the new interest in writing developed the necessary skills for the work of retelling and recording their stories.

So much for the context in which these stories came to be written. But what were the questions they were trying to answer, what issues were troubling these Israelite historians? Essentially, they were grappling with the questions like these:

What *is* Israel?
What were our origins?
What makes us different from other people?

In trying to answer these questions Israel's historians traced the history of their people back to a single family of ancestors, the clan of Abraham. Yet they were also aware that the story was less straightforward than this. The traditions embodied in the books of Joshua and Judges paint another picture—that of a chaotic assortment of different groups from different areas with diverse backgrounds and traditions, rather than one common lineage. And modern scholars have largely confirmed this picture by reconstructing a vivid story of the beginnings of Israel in the banding together of wandering tribesmen, runaway slaves and other social undesirables—all people who were marginal to the life of the comfortable farming communities of the land of Canaan in the 13th and 12th centuries before Christ.

What bound them together was not simply racial kinship or a single strong leader, but something more elusive—a sense of being summoned, taken up, set free by a liberating force beyond themselves. This sense is focused in the memory that they had been slaves and migrant labourers in Egypt, and that their deliverance from Egypt, and the impulse that had led them together into Canaan, came from a God who had chosen them and bound himself to their welfare and interest. They had been unified and given an identity because they were *allied with* this God.

Israel existed, in short, because of their God's commitment to this small and rather messy bundle of human beings—because of an alliance or *covenant* between them and him. 'Covenant' is a word which has for us either vaguely religious or vaguely financial overtones. But the Hebrew word seems originally to have meant 'a solemn public agreement', binding two parties. It could be between individuals, between husband and wife, or between kings or cities. There is a fairly mundane example in Genesis 21: 25–32, where a 'covenant' is made in order to settle a quarrel about where a nomadic group has the right to water its animals, and the word continues to be used in this everyday sense. But, as the Old Testament moves on, it is clear that the chief sense of the word is *God's* treaty: the fact that God has chosen to *make* a people by promising his presence and aid to a group with relatively little natural inner cohesion.

As the people of Israel in later centuries constantly needed to remind themselves, this was a surprising way for a nation to start. At some time in the 8th or 7th century BC, a Hebrew writer with a passionate concern for reform and renewal represents Moses as challenging the people to

> '. . . search into days gone by, long before your time, beginning at the day when God created man on earth, search from one end of heaven to the other, and ask if any deed as mighty as this has been seen or heard. Did any people ever hear the voice of God speaking out of the fire, as you heard it, and remain alive? Or did ever a god attempt to come and take a nation for himself away from another nation, with a challenge, and with signs, portents and wars, with a strong hand and an outstretched arm, and with great deeds of terror, as the LORD your God did for you in Egypt in the sight of you all?'
>
> (Deut. 4: 32–34.)

Later in the same book, Israel is reminded that God's action was 'not because you were more numerous than any other nation' (Deut. 7: 7). Nothing persuades God to do what he does, except his own generous mercy. The covenant is not an agreement between rival powers; although God 'binds' himself in his treaty, it is he who makes the terms. If he did not first speak, the people would not even be there to answer. Their dignity, their independence, above all their creative freedom, owes everything to the initiative of God. In the words of a very ancient formula (Exod. 19: 5–6) Israel is to be God's 'special possession . . . my kingdom of priests, my holy nation'.

But treaties have obligations. God 'obliges' himself in his covenant to be loyal to the people he has chosen and welded together, *and* he lays obligations on that people. They are set free and made holy *for* something. Their status as God's people has to be actively expressed. The Israelite authors put together an account of the *identity* of Israel as the people created by God's choice and promise, and linked it closely with a notion of the *vocation* of Israel. Israel is called to live out its freedom in specific and detailed ways, by keeping God's law. It sounds strange to speak of the Old Testament law as a sign of freedom (partly because we tend to read the New Testament as if it represented a straightforward rejection of the law of the Old); but for the Israelites, the law was a gift. It meant that it was now possible to live a life in accord with the will of God, a life that had shape and order, meaning and dignity. The actions and relationships of daily experience could now be understood as something done for God—a 'sacrifice' offered by the kingdom of priests. All activity became ritualised—more and more in the later books of the Old Testament, like Leviticus—not in such a way that it was burdensome and oppressive, but in order that all of it could be directed towards God.

So when Israel fails to keep the law, God does not desert it, *nor* does he punish simply out of offended dignity or anger. His promise to be loyal to the alliance is anything but a promise to leave Israel 'in peace'. *His* loyalty means that he holds Israel to its side of the treaty, because only in *their* loyalty will they find the real freedom he designs for them. They are not free—as we say—to go to hell in their own way. If God punishes Israel for its failure, it is because he will not allow it to betray itself, its true identity and calling. This is the message of the book of Deuteronomy, and of the writers who edited the history of Israel into its more or less final form in the 7th and 6th centuries BC. This is the history we read in the books of Joshua, Judges, Samuel and Kings. Their work is really the climax of the process that began in the reign of Solomon, the working-out of what the true nature of the Israelite community was.

Summary

Israel's identity and integrity rest on the double foundation of covenant and law, the treaty and its obligations—and so ultimately on God's decision to be Israel's God. He is the guarantor of what Israel is, *and that is both deeply reassuring and deeply disturbing.* He will never cease to challenge his people, at every point in their individual and communal lives. His promise of loyalty is not a licence to Israel to do what it likes because God has promised his mercy. On the contrary, God will never let himself be forgotten by Israel; so long as they reflect at all on who and what they are, they must reckon with him. When they stop reflecting, when they become complacent, about the state of things, God brings disaster on them, to remind them that there is no security for them without loyal obedience. It follows that *integrity* and *security* are inseparable for a community like Israel. With this crucial implication of the covenant in mind we are ready to review the Israelites' experience of trying to preserve their security.

1.3. SECURITY

The conviction that there is no security without integrity points towards the great dilemma repeatedly faced by the Kingdom of Israel and Judah after the age of Solomon. The original state split into two warring groups with rival dynasties, the life of the cities developed more and more rapidly, with all the attendant problems about wealth and poverty, and a succession of enormous and aggressive empires arose on the eastern frontier. The rulers of the two kingdoms could not avoid asking questions about how to stabilise and protect their societies. The problem repeatedly posed by the prophets was this: if the state is protected by military strength, or by the use of wealth and influence to guarantee foreign alliances, this represents a compromising of the people's loyalty to God.

There is a dramatic example in 2 Kings 16. The southern kingdom of Judah is threatened by the larger northern state, Israel and its ally, Aram; Ahaz, King of Judah, appeals to the 'superpower' of the day, the empire of Assyria, and buys the friendship of the Assyrian King with gifts taken from the Jerusalem temple. He even revises the ritual of the temple to conform a bit more closely with what Assyria demanded of its vassals. If we turn from this passage to the famous seventh chapter of Isaiah, we can see how the crisis appeared to those in Jerusalem most deeply concerned with the religious integrity of the state. Isaiah encourages Ahaz not to trust in any foreign power but only in God, whose purpose and action will appear as time goes on. Isaiah assures the King that rescue will come; but the hard fact is that he is exhorting Ahaz to take a political risk rather than sacrifice the state's faithfulness to God.

The prophets saw that the problem of preserving Israel's integrity ran far deeper than simply the conduct of its defence policies and external relations. Such policies could easily compromise the Israelites' obligations and calling under the covenant—and frequently they did. But they were not the only ways in which the integrity of the community might be eroded. Its own internal organisation—its religious, political and social institutions—had to continue to reflect Israel's special calling, existing only on God's mercy as a model of just and free life together. Only by keeping the covenant and the law can the people of Israel be assured of God's protection. If they become complacent and allow injustice and oppression to creep back into their way of life then they no longer are assured of, nor deserve, God's protection.

To see the full implications of this it is important to understand that, as time went on, many Israelites had come to see the Royal House of David as something established by covenant, as an essential feature of their society (2 Sam. 7, Ps. 89, etc.). Likewise the Royal City of Jerusalem and the temple were 'sacraments' of God's presence among his people (e.g. Pss. 46 and 48). It is clear from Isaiah and Jeremiah that there were those who believed that all this implied the invulnerability of Jerusalem, that the city could never be captured or overthrown. As long as they preserved these institutions, God's protection was assured.

The prophets thought otherwise. For example, Jeremiah, chapters 34–44, is a narrative depicting the fall of the southern kingdom (587–6 BC) to the Babylonians; and it portrays the prophet as an unmistakable threat to the morale of the nation. As elsewhere in the book, Jeremiah proclaims as his 'word from the Lord' God's *refusal* to save Judah as an independent state.

God is not concerned with the survival of Israel and Judah as independent political units like other kingdoms, but with the survival of a community representing his freedom and justice; and the existence of such a community does not necessarily depend on any one set of political institutions. This, of course, was a major challenge to the ideas of the Hebrew kings—whose survival was certainly not guaranteed in Jeremiah's scheme of things!

He utterly denies (Jer. 7: 9 – 15) the idea that the presence of the temple in Jerusalem will protect the city when the justice and integrity of the covenant community have disappeared, and the whole burden of Jeremiah's message in the last days of the Kingdom is that God makes no promise to protect either the shrine or the royal house.

Implicit in much of this is a critique of kingship itself. Hosea 8: 4 complains how, in the northern kingdom of the 8th century, kingship had become debased. The people thought of it 'as an institution whose management was their prerogative . . . a focus of power independent of Yahweh' (C. J. L. Mays, *Hosea* SCM 1969, p.117). Kingship had ceased to be a kind of spiritual leadership and had become a tool for power-hungry men.

Even harsher is the picture given in 1 Samuel 8 – 12, where Samuel passes on to the people God's judgment on them for having asked for a king at all. The demand for a king, 'like other nations' (8: 5) implies a rejection of the true kingship of God, and of the charismatic guidance of a 'judge' or a prophet. Israel ceases to define itself as God's community and struggles to become just another competitor in the political rat-race. The traditions preserved in these chapters are very ancient, but they are presented to us in a work composed probably in the 6th century BC, when hindsight had intensified the feeling that the monarchy might have been a wrong turning in Israel's history. Israel has, again, been seeking to secure its status as a 'real' nation by means which compromise its integrity.

If it protects itself by adopting the oppressive forms of sacred monarchy or by building up its military power, or by bribing its way to influential alliances, it has made itself not worth protecting, in God's eyes. As a *state* it must take its chance in the jungle warfare of politics, without any divine guarantee of protection, and in so far as it accepts unrest, tyranny and inequality in its internal life, it becomes less likely to survive even on these terms.

Jeremiah sums this up in his famous 'parable of the potter' (Jer. 18: 1 – 12). God can and will do as he likes with the nations: if a nation is disobedient to him, he is free to abandon it to its fate. The implication (worked out later in Chapter 3) is that *Israel does not have to be an independent nation in order to be God's people*. It may be that it can exist under various political systems without ceasing to be itself or losing the promised friendship and intimacy with God—its foundation is the conviction of God's closeness, loyalty and love.

For these reasons, after the fall of Jerusalem, the prophet condemns in God's name both those who seek by armed resistance to break the regime established after the conquest, and those hoping to flee to Egypt in order to avoid the harsh and uncertain circumstances of life in an occupied country. What God demands is an acceptance of what was happened and a commitment to reassured faithfulness in new conditions. This may sound like defeatism, but actually it is a message of hope: if the people of Israel turn back to God, he will renew his friendship and support for them. Jeremiah is reaffirming the significance of the covenant—there is hope even in defeat.

Summary

This section has been a swift and brief survey of ancient Israel's search for security through political, military and diplomatic efforts, and the discovery that none of these could guarantee security—indeed, they frequently undermined it. Worse still, the Israelites could not even take for granted that the continuation of their traditional religious practices and institutions would ensure God's favour. So what were they supposed to do? It is time to consider the implications of Israel's experience.

1.4. LIVING WITH THE DILEMMA OF SECURITY

So far, in considering how the Israelites attempted to preserve their identity, we have dealt with the various mistakes and failings exposed so bluntly by the prophets. But what are the positive lessons to be learned from all this? What, actually, do the authors of the Old Testament seem to be saying that the Israelites should do instead? The answer is, in a sense, simple: they should keep the covenant—that is, *really* keep it—and they should trust in the Lord. But it is important to be clear what this implies.

Given the prophets' condemnations of military force, diplomatic alliances, the monarchy and the existing religious institutions, it is easy to make the mistake of thinking that all these are, as such, irrelevant or worse. After all, didn't Jeremiah suggest that the Israelites could serve God under alien rule? But the prophets were not saying anything of the sort, for this would amount to relegating religion to a matter of private devotions and personal conduct. These were important, of course, but the covenant called for much more than this—a community life that reflected God's justice and liberating will.

No, the prophets were recommending something more difficult. It was not a matter of ignoring the state's external relations, but of conducting them in a way consistent with Israel's identity and calling. It was not a matter of ignoring political (and religious) institutions, but of ensuring that they remained faithful to the covenant and the law. It was not that alien rule was unimportant, but rather a matter of accepting the loss, and finding new ways of living out God's purpose.

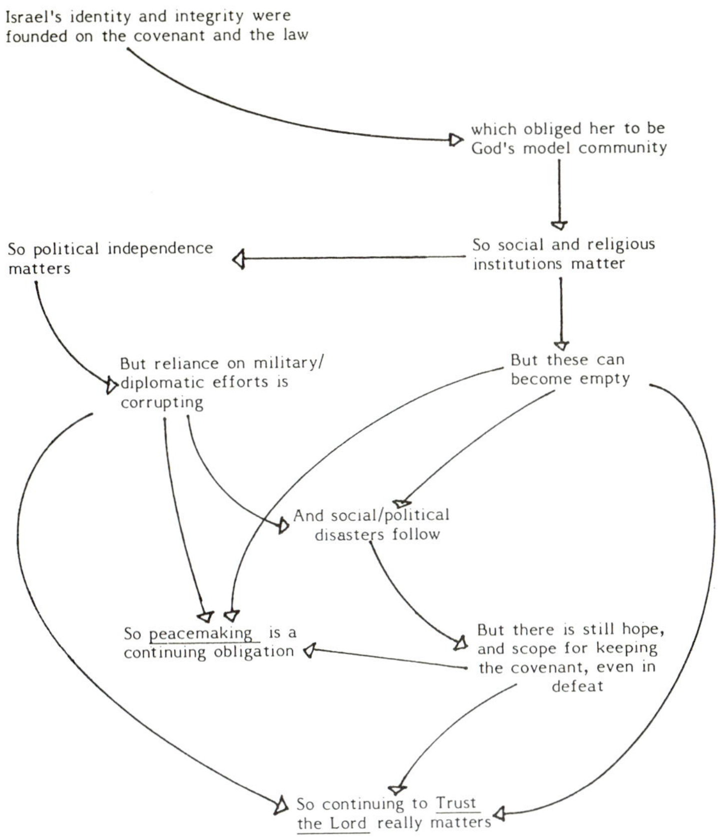

Figure 2. Summary of Chapter 1.

So the prophets were not calling on the people of Israel to abandon politics as a dirty business, but to recognise it as another, and vital, arena in which to fulfil their calling. In more practical terms, this meant that, both as regards the neighbouring kingdoms and as regards the divisions in their own society, they were obliged to be *peacemakers*. Only by pursuing peace in public affairs (as well as private life) would they be consistent with their identity as God's chosen people.

The ideas of peace and peacemaking are in fact central themes in the Old and the New Testaments so they need to be dealt with separately. The next chapter examines more closely what this obligation to engage in peacemaking involves.

The other implication that comes out clearly from ancient Israel's often misdirected efforts to achieve security is the need to trust in the Lord. Again this can easily be misunderstood as a politically naive and reckless policy amounting, in effect, to wishful thinking. But the prophets knew perfectly well that their proposals involved major political risks. They, however, were thinking longer term; they saw where the policies they criticised were leading. And they understood that *any* policy involved risks: Israel's security could not be guaranteed by military or diplomatic efforts, since those efforts involved compromising Israel's commitment to the covenant. So whatever the Israelites did would be risky—the only difference being that the risks the prophets recommended taking were more obvious. The consequences of trusting in the Lord might not be *immediately* rewarding, but in the end God would support and restore his people if they were faithful to him.

The idea of trusting in the Lord is one that will be developed in more detail in Chapter 3. For the meantime, Figure 2 represents a summary of the story so far.

1.5. THE DILEMMA TODAY

As we have seen, security posed a dilemma for the Israelites because, under the covenant, what they had to protect was not just their territorial integrity and political independence, but the integrity of their community life as an expression of God's freedom and justice. As a result, whatever efforts they made (including not making an effort—giving up) ran the constant risk of undermining precisely what they were attempting to protect.

The relevance for us today is not hard to spot. We may think of ourselves as the 'New Israel' of the Christian Church, struggling to respond to the sense of God's undeserved acceptance, and to express in our day-to-day life the shape of a society marked by God's love; or we may think of Britain as a society whose basic identity is bound up with a commitment to ideals of freedom, social justice and democracy. In either case, security must mean more than simply preserving existing institutional arrangements at all costs. *The question of security cannot be separated from the question of our own integrity.* And that means we too face the dilemma of security—attempts to protect what we value can easily erode precisely those values.

Given that this is so, the implications for us are the same as for the Israelites: our foreign and domestic policies have to be consistent with our identity, with the values we consider essential to our way of life. We, too, are obliged to undertake continuing efforts at peacemaking. Likewise, we must also trust in the Lord. We shouldn't imagine that we can play it safe, and avoid taking any risks over national security, for every policy has its risks. So it's a question of *which* risks we are going to take—and how far are we prepared to trust that in the long term, in the uncertain world of power politics, developing the integrity of our community offers the best prospect for ensuring the survival and the realisation of our ideals.

But how does all this actually apply to our current situation? What are the practical implications of the Bible's teaching on this issue? That is something we must all try to work out for ourselves, for it remains our responsibility to live God's life as best we can. The Bible offers guidance, not a detailed set of instructions for every eventuality; and it is up to us to work out the implications of that guidance for our own time. So in the remainder of this chapter, there are some questions and examples to set you thinking about the implications, as you see them, of the dilemma of security we have been considering. It should be possible to say, in effect, 'I don't think this policy does jeopardise our integrity, yet—but if we went *that* far, then it certainly would!' The point is that unless we can say what *would* be going too far, then our position is still that of saying: security at all costs. That position ignores the dilemma identified by the prophets—the fact that one cannot treat national security on its own. It is intimately bound up with national *integrity*.

Questions and examples for discussion

(a) Which of the following statements better reflects the Old Testament view of the relationship between national security and national integrity?

— 'national security is essential to preserve one's integrity'
— 'national integrity is essential to preserve one's security'

How much of each do you think underlies discussions of security nowadays?

(b) In the mid 1970s the then Labour Government committed more than £1000 million to modernising the guidance systems of the missiles in Britain's nuclear submarines, even though the Labour Party was committed to nuclear disarmament. This decision was taken neither to the Cabinet, nor to Parliament. It became public knowledge some years later. Was this an erosion of democracy? If so, was it necessary to protect democracy? If not, how far can secrecy in matters of defence and public expenditure go before democracy does start to be eroded?

(c) As well as the thousands of millions of pounds committed to defence, it has been estimated that over half of our trained scientists and engineers work on defence-related projects. Is this compatible with our declared commitments to social justice and peace? If so, how much of our national resources are we willing to commit to defence? What other costs—in terms, perhaps, of social conflict and unrest, poverty and reduced welfare services—is it right to bear? How do we make that decision?

(d) It often seems to be suggested that a Russian invasion would be the ultimate disaster. A Russian invasion is certainly not an appealing prospect, but let us *consider* the possibility of struggling to preserve our values under an occupying power. What might be a worse possibility than a period of foreign rule? Unless we want to ignore the dilemma by saying 'territorial integrity at all costs', we have to consider the sort of conditions (however remote they may be at present) under which we might say 'if this is what preserving our political independence requires, then it's simply not worth it'. What do you consider would make it 'not worth it'—if anything?

Further study

(a) Covenant. It may be useful to follow through the records of different *kinds* of covenant in the Old Testament, from the promise to Noah—and so to all humanity (in Genesis 9: 1 – 17, quite a late text, in fact)—to the promise to Abraham (Gen. 17: 1 – 22), and then the classical accounts of the covenant made through the mediation of Moses at Mount Sinai, in passages like Exodus 19: 1 – 8, 24: 1 – 8, 34: 5 – 33; Deuteronomy 4: 44 – 6: 3, 28: 1 – 29: 1, and the renewal of the agreement in the presence of Joshua (Jos. 24: 1 – 28). You might consider how the *scope* of the covenant varies, and how promise and obligation are interwoven in these texts.

(b) Security. As suggested in Section 1.3, the crisis recorded in 2 Kings 16 and Isaiah 7: 1 – 17 is a good place to start. Of the relevant sections of the book of Jeremiah, Chapters 37 and 42 are particularly clear.

Attitudes to kingship are reflected in Deuteronomy 17: 14 – 20 (a warning put into the mouth of Moses by a writer disillusioned with the sort of monarchy represented by Solomon and his successors—effectively a return to captivity in Egypt), Judges 9 (a first disastrous experiment) and the passages referred to from 1 Samuel 8 – 12.

Alliances with any power other than God are a regular target for prophetic criticism. Isaiah 31 condemns 'those who go down to Egypt for help', and Hosea repeatedly castigates the northern kingdom's chaotic foreign and defence policies as being an aspect of that state's general 'wantonness' and 'adultery'. See, for example, Hosea 5: 13; 7: 8 – 16; 8: 9 – 15; 11: 5; 12: 1; 14: 3.

CHAPTER 2

What is peace?

2.1. INTRODUCTION

In Chapter 1 we saw how the Israelites faced the dilemma of national security, and discovered it to be bound up in their identity as God's chosen people. Part of the resolution of their dilemma was the realisation that the covenant relationship required them to work to make peace. This chapter takes a look at the two great biblical words for peace:

- in the Old Testament, the Hebrew word SHALOM;
- in the New Testament, the Greek word EIRENE.

We shall examine the strikingly wide range of meanings of these words by looking at particular texts which show what these words meant to the people who used them. At the end of each section a question for discussion will relate the biblical ideas to a present-day issue.

What we hope will emerge is a direct challenge to any negative or static ideas of what peace is. Peace is not just the absence of conflict.

The discussion of *shalom* will show that peace is inseparable from justice; and this involves us in all kinds of hard questions about how people are to live together in any kind of community. A community could be a family, a street, a church, a city, a nation, or indeed, the world. To create *shalom* in the human community is more than just a balancing of tensions, or of keeping hostilities in check.

Some uses of *eirene* in the New Testament are very close to the concept of *shalom* (this is particularly true in the gospels). Elsewhere in the New Testament we find a different use of the word, specifically linked to breaking boundaries and effecting reconciliation, with God and with other human beings.

What will emerge will be some sense of balance between the two concepts. *Shalom* is concerned primarily with the internal life of a community, its justice and balance. *Eirene* points a little more in the direction of activity to extend the life of the community and to make it available to all.

2.2. PEACE AND WHOLENESS

The most primitive meaning of *shalom* seems to be something like 'completeness' or 'wholeness'. *Shalom* in Hebrew is a noun related to a similar verb, whose meanings are, in various forms, 'to be healthy'; 'to finish or complete some action'; 'to keep a promise'; 'to restore something taken away'; or even (rather surprisingly) 'to take revenge' or 'pay someone back'. Examples of these meanings (in order) may be found in Leviticus 22: 21, Isaiah 19: 21, Exodus 22: 3 (and also 2 Samuel 12: 6), 2 Kings 9: 26. Remember that in the original Hebrew, each of these concepts is in fact a *shalom* word, a fact which is not obvious to us reading the English text. The first thing to notice in all these cases is that the authors assume that there exists a normal and balanced order of things which has been, or could be, upset. This balanced order could mean (as in the texts referred to):

- the health of the flesh of an animal for sacrifice;
- the moral order;
- the proper and truthful relation between word and deed, promise and performance;
- the order of relationships disrupted by violent offences which have passed without justice being reaffirmed.

It is also worth noting that the word for a thanksgiving sacrifice is another member of the *shalom* group (there is an example of this in 2 Chronicles 33: 16). A failure to complete or finish a stage in the relationship between us and God, by giving appropriate thanks, is another way of rupturing the order of things.

Shalom is therefore a word for a 'right order' which may be upset or broken by any number of things. It is a dynamic, not a static order. It is like the orderliness of a living organism which constantly adapts itself to its environment, grows and changes. In one sense this order is indestructible. It may be damaged, it may become covered up, but it is still there. It provides the point of reference and the impulse to work for it being 'mended' and 'uncovered' again. In another sense this order is profoundly vulnerable, because it requires unfailing and unceasing attention from the human beings who are striving to live in accord with it. It is an order in which God is involved. God is ultimately the source of that pressure on us which impels us to act for the sake of restoring and perfecting the world, and of creating a just community.

It is significant that we have no single word in English to capture this range of meanings. We are not alone in this. Our culture, like many others, has lost a sense of humanity as an integral part of nature. So it is not surprising that we are short of words that express a *wholeness* in the created order. The importance of attempting to understand the Hebrew concept of *shalom* is that it may prompt us to wonder how we as Christians are to cope with a society like ours, when we are committed to a tradition which seeks 'peace' in the all embracing sense of the Old Testament word.

For discussion

Israel was called to make peace both within itself as a community, and also beyond its confines as a nation. The Christian Church is likewise called to make peace, internally and externally.

Do you think that the lack of Church unity shows our failure to make peace within the Church? If you think so, what steps do you think the Church should be taking at both national and local levels?

What steps could we take to create *shalom* within the Church as a whole, within our own denomination, and within our own congregation?

2.3. PEACE AND PROSPERITY

The phrase 'peace and prosperity' is a cliché, which can often sound rather like 'safety to make money' and not much more. In the Old Testament, however, prosperity is always God's gift, and is to be acknowledged as such. Otherwise it becomes an occasion for disobedience, or forgetfulness of God. Thus prosperity can never be an end in itself—it must always mean the full flourishing of human beings under God.

Look at Isaiah 26: 12. The prophet here expresses his hope that the Lord will give *shalom*, in the sense of prosperity. It is in the context of the hope for deliverance from bondage and disgrace. God will remove the obstacles to human wholeness, obstacles of violence and injustice, and the shame involved in the fall and captivity of Israel. God will enable the people to flourish once again.

Look at Psalm 85. This psalm celebrates the restoration of Israel's fortunes and describes God (see verse 8) speaking words of *shalom* to the people. The 'words of peace' are a promise of abundance and wealth—but abundance and wealth inseparable from the active presence of God, and inseparable from justice (see verse 10).

What we have said so far about peace and prosperity has been applied to the life of the whole community of Israel, but the same is true of the life of the individual.

Look at Job 22: 21. One of Job's unhelpful comforters tells him to 'come to terms with God and you will prosper; that is the way to mend your fortune'. Here 'prosper' is another of the words linked with *shalom*. Prosperity, or fortune, depends on just and right relation with God. We tend to read this as a rather crude linking of wealth with virtue, and it is true that the Old Testament can be embarrassingly blunt in its approach to self-interest as a moral motive. However, there is more to it than that. In this passage, Eliphaz has just accused Job of fraud and oppression, implying that his previous 'prosperity' had been bought at the expense of the weak and defenceless. The message is, therefore, that such wealth, because it is not the Lord's gift but the result of human intrigue, is not, and cannot be, real or lasting.

In other words, what this passage is saying very clearly is that if wealth for its own sake is the goal, then it can never be securely possessed. But if justice is pursued for its own sake (and not for hope of reward) then God will give prosperity as well. It is another example of *shalom* as the right ordering of things.

This now links with one of the ideas explored in Chapter 1. There we saw that to pursue security or survival for its own sake, as the overriding goal, will in fact destroy the balance and integrity of communal life. Risk insecurity for the sake of justice, and you will discover God's security. Here we have a similar message about wealth. In both cases there is no *shalom* without justice.

Shalom, then, can mean prosperity; but that prosperity is the flourishing of human beings in the context of the universal order of God's will which is a will making for justice and equity. It is the state that people enjoy when slavery and oppression are removed. Israel's 'peace' is something which can be longed and prayed for, but it cannot be worked for in isolation from the universal quest for justice.

Peacemaking is prosperity-making, but the link between the two (in biblical terms) should make us attend very carefully and critically indeed to what we think 'prosperity' means.

For discussion

We in the rich Northern Hemisphere of the earth enjoy a material standard of living far greater than that of the peoples of the poor South. Because of the state of the world economic order, we enjoy our wealth *at the expense of* the world's poor nations. Has this anything at all to do with the *justice* of which the Old Testament speaks? If not, our material wealth cannot be said to be *prosperity* in the sense used in this section—i.e. a gift from God, but requiring justice. In this case, what can we do to create the justice necessary if our wealth is to be true prosperity?

2.4. PEACE AND JUSTICE

Love and fidelity have come together;
justice and peace join hands.
(Ps. 85: 10)

As in the previous section, here in Psalm 85 we see the *shalom* of God's people restored to their land. It is a peace intertwined with righteousness.

Compare this with Isaiah 32: 16 – 17:

> Then justice shall make its home in the wilderness
> and righteousness dwell in the grassland—
> when righteousness shall yield peace
> and its fruits be quietness and confidence for ever.

This 'righteousness' or justice is the Hebrew word *tsedaqah*—the way of life indicated by the law. The way in which Israel participates in the right order (*shalom*) of things is by obedience to the law; thus *tsedaqah* can also mean right relation with God. So when God looks to the people to create justice and they fail, their relationship with him is damaged. When justice is lacking on earth, there is no peace between God and humanity.

An example of this is found in Jeremiah, where he accuses the priests and prophets of pretending there is *shalom* where there is not:

> They dress my people's wound, but skin-deep only
> with their saying, 'All is well'.
> All well? Nothing is well!
>
> (Jer. 6: 14; 8: 11)

Compare Ezekiel 13: 10, 16. Ezekiel is saying the same thing. Those who speak of *shalom* where there is none are like builders trying to hold a wall together with whitewash.

The prophets agree that people *talk* as if there is 'peace', wholeness or righteousness; but this is totally disconnected from God's claim on us. Part of the prophet's painful task in society is to break down the false appearances of stability and consensus, so as to force our attention once again upon the true nature of *shalom*.

One of the most important lessons from this section is that it is impossible to imagine an ancient Israelite speaking about 'peace with God' except as a part of the health of the people as a whole. This doesn't mean that 'peace with God' is reduced to some earthly state of affairs—because God remains God, the timeless act of grace and gift on which everything depends. But it is important to realise that there is no way, in the language of the Old Testament, to separate salvation, prosperity, justice and peace. Note too, that justice (*tsedaqah*) in this list, can in some contexts mean 'compassion', and 'forgiveness'; it is not a hard, legalistic idea.

For both the individual and the community, all these states or qualities are utterly inseparable. 'Peace with God' was never, for the ancient Israelites, a matter of private thoughts and emotions.

For discussion

The biblical use of *shalom* indicates that there can be no peace without justice. Do you think it is possible to have justice without peace? If not, can you explain why? If you think it is possible, can you give an example?

It is said that nuclear deterrence has 'kept the peace' since 1945. Bearing in mind that *shalom* is a *positive* state of affairs, and requires there to be justice, would you say that the nuclear deterrence has maintained *shalom*, or would you say it has maintained only an absence of open warfare? Can you give reasons or examples to back up your opinions?

2.5. PEACE AND ACTION

It is clear from the preceding sections that *shalom* is not a word that we can easily associate with passivity or resignation. 'Peace' does not mean the absence of something but very plainly means the presence of forceful and critical action. It is injustice, violence and war that represent an absence, a refusal of God's *shalom*. Thus the search for peace is not a withdrawal into private tranquility, an escape from confrontation or from the risks involved in defending justice. If we realise this, then we must challenge *both* sides of the contemporary debate about peace and its preservation:

(a) The official defence policies of the world's most heavily armed states make much of the 'peacemaking' effect of nuclear weapons. They have 'preserved the peace' by the fact that the cost of conflict, in terms of destruction, devastation and loss of life, has become unacceptably high. After reading this chapter so far, we might wish to join the prophets in their savage complaint:

> All well? Nothing is well!

This view of 'peace' preserved by the nuclear arsenals of the powerful nations is a *negative* view of peace; so it is not surprising that it exists side by side with unjust and divided societies—on both 'sides' of the arms race, and in the remainder of the poor nations of the earth. Debates about defence policy are totally unrelated to national or international debates about economic justice. As we have seen, there can be no *shalom* unless these issues become central.

Considerations of human rights or civil liberties similarly are not central, as they must be if we are to create *shalom*. Rather, they have become pawns, occasions for scoring debating points, in the game of power politics.

Then there is the question of the health of our society as a whole—again central to the making of *shalom*. If we judge that, overall, we do not live in a healthy society, we must, surely, lay some of that at the door of the arms race—both because of its very high economic cost, and perhaps even more significantly because of the creeping fatalism, anxiety, and sense of powerlessness felt by many as a result of it.

To talk about humanity as fallen and sinful, and to say that therefore an unhealthy society is to be expected, is not a very adequate response to the situation. For one thing, it ignores all that we have learned so far about God's commitment to our health and wholeness, as shown by his claims on Israel. There is no doubt evidence for sin everywhere—but that is no reason for inactivity. Where sin is the cause of a lack of *shalom*, then our task is not to accept that, but to work to create *shalom*.

(b) The argument cuts both ways, of course. There are some in the peace movements who speak and write as if the avoidance of nuclear conflict were the only important issue claiming our loyalty, time and attention. In other words, they accept the negative definition of peace offered by those in power. They are evading the difficult question:

> *Is there *anything* which would make conflict, armed conflict, unavoidable for an honest person?

Even if the answer is that there is nothing, absolutely nothing, that would make a nuclear exchange acceptable, then the peace movements still have to make clear that their option for 'peace' would be an option for justice, rather than complacency, in the face of a possible threat of, say, appalling tyranny. This takes us back to the question explored in Chapter 1, about what happens to the justice of a community when it is defended by unjust means.

For discussion

Do you think that governments show enough concern about the social consequences of their defence policies? For instance, as with Israel, does maintaining our national security threaten our identity, integrity or inner cohesiveness?

Do you think that peace campaigners show enough concern for justice when they call for a change of defence policies? For instance, are they opting out of the global struggle for liberty and righteousness?

What is your opinion on the question posed at * above?

2.6. PEACE IN THE NEW TESTAMENT

Of all the gospels, it is perhaps Luke's which most interestingly weaves the theme of peace into the whole story. A passage from Luke's gospel, known to many people who rarely, if ever, set foot inside a church, is the angels' song:

> Glory to God in highest heaven, and on earth
> peace for men on whom his favour rests
> (Luke 2: 14)

This is the translation given in the New English Bible, though the message is doubtless better known in the many versions in which it is used in Christmas carols. What is the nature of the 'peace' in this passage?

Read Luke 1: 46–55, Mary's great and famous hymn, and compare it with Luke 1: 68–79. Here Zechariah looks forward to the dawning on us of God's compassion, 'to shine on those who live in darkness, under the cloud of death, and to guide our feet into the way of peace'. It is these ideas of peace that the angels' song is echoing. In the light of the hymns of Mary and Zechariah, it is clear that the peace brought by Jesus is definitely not the cosy calmness that the word sometimes conjures up (especially at Christmas!). This peace is the triumph of God's justice. It is God's casting in his lot with the oppressed and the captives, God's restoration of the fortunes of his people.

Read Luke 2: 25–32, the Song of Simeon. Simeon, we are told, 'watched and waited for the restoration of Israel', and in this passage we see him welcoming Jesus, who gives him leave to 'go in peace'. This is not a peace of calm resignation, but a joyful confidence that Israel has at last been empowered to fulfil its calling to gather all the nations together under God. Yet it is also Simeon who warns Mary that 'this child is destined to be a sign which men reject' (Luke 2: 34).

So, as for the prophets before, the peace of a restored and liberated Israel is to be found on the far side of bitter conflict with the forces of injustice and unpeacefulness. Luke's nativity story makes the role of Jesus as the bringer of peace to Israel quite clear. At the same time it is made clear that the coming of *God's* peace may mean the disruption of the existing peace.

Read Luke 12: 51 and Matthew 10: 34. Jesus' remark, 'Do you think that I came to establish peace on earth?' is spoken with a heavy irony. We should hear that irony—characteristic of many of Jesus' sayings—as a note of warning. We must go back to examine what we mean by 'peace', and ask ourselves whether we have heard the angels' message as just a comfortable, consoling one.

Now read Luke 19: 28–48. Here the irony is in the whole event. The people welcome Jesus with the cry, 'Peace in heaven, glory in highest heaven!' (v. 38). This looks superficially like the angels' song, but this time earth has been forgotten. The people look for heavenly peace to descend, but they do not grasp what peace on earth might mean. So in verse 42, we find Jesus weeping over the city, and saying "If only you had known, on this great day, the way that leads to peace!'.

That way of peace is a path that Jesus must tread alone. Israel will refuse that path, and refuse him. It will seek its *shalom*, its security, by some means other than the vulnerable trust that God's way demands. So it will perish like the old kingdom before it. Because Israel misunderstands *shalom*, it cannot recognise 'God's moment' (see verse 44), the time of immediacy and urgency, the time of the approach of the kingdom. It cannot hear that good news, because it cannot risk the conflict and the suffering of God's peace. So we can see that Luke weaves the idea of *shalom* into the whole of his story, from beginning to end.

The next section will turn to other parts of the New Testament to discover what they have to say about *eirene*.

Peace with God

By the time we get to Paul's letters, we are a considerable distance away from the words of Jesus. Paul's use of *eirene* is often in the more prosaic sense of good order and calm—'peace and quiet', as we might say. However, we need to look more seriously at other uses of *eirene* in Paul and in the rest of the New Testament writers before jumping to the conclusion that we have here a recipe for passivity and quietism.

Paul writes often about our peace with God, a peace brought about by God's initiative. God has overcome the state of enmity between the world and himself and has created the peace which is reconciliation. Look at Romans 5 and 2 Corinthians 5 for examples of this.

What kind of 'peace' is this? When we are 'safe' by our own lights, we are in fact at risk because we have shut God out and made him our 'enemy'. The gospel speaks of 'God's peace' and 'peace with God' in a way that is a challenge to us. It is a challenge, a question, that must always undermine our understanding of the peace we *think* we have. If that is a peace without God, it is no peace.

The promise of peace with God through faith is as unsettling as the rest of the gospel. If taken seriously, it forces us to ask whether what we are content with ('at peace' with) is *God's* order and the stability of God's love—or whether it is a worldly security, based on defence and exclusion, and thus on fear and sin. 'Love, joy, peace, patience' are among the gifts of the Spirit (Gal. 5: 22). This kind of peace is precisely the opposite of the spirit of worldly peace (propped up by fear), because it is so intimately connected with trusting love.

Paul writes mostly about what stifles the life of the Kingdom in the individual; but of course this shows itself also in the breakdown of community life. God is a peacemaking, a reconciling God. If we claim to have peace with him while finding ourselves incapable of patience with each other, then it is fair enough to ask *what* God we are at peace with! A 'peaceful' community could be one that is merely so rigid and static that nothing happens at all. This is not what the biblical writers mean by 'peace'. God's peace, as realised through the Easter event, is a judgement on the various bargains we strike with life—a judgement on our readiness to be content with less than the truth, on our incapacity to grow painfully and riskily into the wholeness he promises.

As in the Old Testament, 'peace with God', cannot be reduced to the state of mind of an individual. Understanding it, being able to know whether it is present or absent, depends on being able to see how God's grace is part and parcel of the life of faith—and that means being open and vulnerable to the signs of the Kingdom wherever they may be found.

For discussion

Do you think that it is possible to find signs of the Kingdom outside the Church? If so, can you give some examples? If not, can you say why you think it is not possible?

Peace across frontiers

Read Ephesians 2: 11–19: these words could serve as a summary of the whole argument of this book. The new covenant is brought into being by the Cross, and breaks the mould of the ancient definition of the covenant people. Now the law no longer stands as the sign of the superiority or the exclusivity of God's people. It is swept away to give place to the fundamental purpose that God has had from all eternity, and which the law once symbolised. A new humanity, a new covenant people, is to assemble round the one obedient son of the covenant. All this is *making peace.*

Look at Colossians 3: 11: this reminds us that the gospel sweeps away all national, cultural and class divisions. To be members of Christ's body is to be called to his peace, and there is no escape from this call. It is based on two fundamental truths:

1. *within* the Church, no one has a right to opt out of the life of mutual love: no one can seriously live in the Church with their nationalist, traditionalist or class superiorities intact.
2. *beyond* the Church, no one may be regarded as 'without hope and without God' for good and all, purely because of some worldly circumstances.

There are no areas of the human world or human experience that the gospel can ignore, and no human being to whom we can assume it is irrelevant. So, if we are incorporated into the peacemaking activity of Christ by our baptismal faith, we are to engage in the process of crossing barriers, of taking peace to those far off—because that is in itself an aspect of our own peace.

For discussion

Read again point (1) above. Do you think the long-established denominations in this country have offered enough love and acceptance to the newer black Pentecostalist Churches? If not, what could be done about this?

Read again point (2) above. Do you think that we are sometimes in danger of regarding the people (other than the Christians) of the Soviet Union and Eastern Europe as 'without hope'?

Summary

In this chapter we have considered the Old Testament concept of *shalom* and the New Testament usage of *eirene*. In both cases it is clear that what is meant in the Bible by 'peace' is not primarily an individual's emotions, or attitudes towards life. Peace is to be sought and created in the context of God's order, of wholeness in individuals and in the community, of justice and of the flourishing of the whole of humanity.

The questions for discussion at the end of each section have, we hope, helped to make it clear that these concepts of peace are important tools for us. They can help us to make sense of the political and ethical debates about peace, security and defence that are so vital at this time.

The Further Study section which follows opens up some of the larger dimensions of the questions we have considered in this chapter.

Further study

(a) **Prosperity**. Deuteronomy 6 and 8, classic texts on covenant obligation, which emphasises the gift to Israel of the land and its resources, might be a starting point for considering the idea of prosperity as a gift and the risks involved in separating prosperity from the covenant relationship in its entirety. This could also be usefully linked with the questions about security raised in Chapter 1.

(b) **The cosmic order**. In addition to the passages mentioned in the main text, Amos 5: 4–15 and Psalms 119: 89–112; 145; 146; and 147 treat the relation between the covenant demands and the stable order of the universe in a variety of ways. The question posed for us is whether we think of 'right behaviour' primarily as conforming to an external command or as a kind of participation in a universal harmony.

(c) **Church and creation**. Ephesians 1–4 and Colossians 1: 1–2; 15 are very important in the development of a Christian theology of 'new creation'. They might therefore be used in thinking about human responsibility in the new order for the *non*-human creation. Is it sentimentality to raise the question of 'peace' in relation to our use of the world's material resources, or our attitudes to the animal world? How much of the world is involved in the supposedly universal peace flowing from Christ's work?

Another issue connected with these passages is that of the 'powers' enslaving us, standing between us and God. For the first century, they were angels, gods, demons; what are the modern equivalents? Systems of ideas, social structures? Or do we still need a language which speaks of 'supernatural' forces holding back peace and freedom?

(d) Insiders and outsiders. Jesus had to cope with the savage hostility of Jews to Samaritans. Paul in Galatians 3: 28 (cf. Col. 3: 11) sees the important divisions as those between 'Jew and Greek, slave and freeman, male and female'. What are the important divisions now? And what groups or types of person do we now think of instinctively as 'outsiders' from the Church's point of view—political rebels, sexual offenders, financial frauds, the young, the single?

CHAPTER 3

In God we trust

3.1. INTRODUCTION

Chapter 1 concluded with two main points:

(i) one solution to Israel's dilemma over security and identity was to love and trust God;
(ii) an obligation on Israel as God's chosen people, his model community, was the continuing work of making peace.

Chapter 2 examined the nature of this 'peace'—*shalom*—that Israel was to make, and explored how that concept of peace changed and developed during the New Testament era—the idea of *eirene*.

In this chapter we turn to Israel's 'trust in God'. We examine what it meant for the ancient Israelites, and what it means for the Christian Church today. In addition, we show how trusting God, being part of the covenant community, cannot be separated from the work of creating *shalom* in the world.

The Old Testament understanding of trust in God is that it is part of the covenant relationship between God and Israel. That covenant is about living in right relationship with God, and thus creating *shalom*. So Section 3.2 examines Israel's way of trusting God and what that has to teach us. From there we move on, in Section 3.3, to explore the ideas of the new covenant—ideas present in the Old Testament and fulfilled, as Paul and the writers of the gospels tell us, in the person of Jesus. This section brings us to the realisation that the continuing of God's purpose does not depend on the maintaining of any particular political system, nor any particular nation (not even Israel). The continuing of God's purpose is to be found in the response of each of us in our hearts, and in our working *together* to create 'a new heaven and a new earth'.

The overall structure of this chapter, in relation to Chapters 1 and 2, may be summarised as follows:

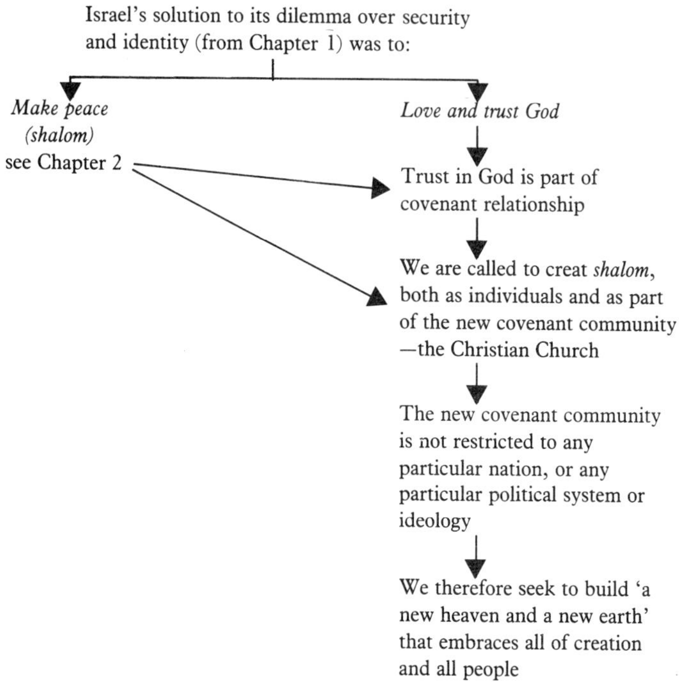

3.2. ISRAEL SHOWS THE MEANING OF TRUST

The ancient Israelites saw that part of the solution to their dilemma about security and identity was to love and trust God: this love and trust were in the context of God's covenant with them. God had a special relationship with the people of Israel, and their part of the 'bargain' was to be faithful to God—and faith includes loving and trusting.

However, God's gift of his fellowship to Israel was not a thing to be 'hoarded' or exploited by the people to their own advantage. Like all God's gifts, it was part of the whole divine activity, the drawing together of his creation into harmony with himself. His purposes were not limited to Israel, and the special relationship between Israel and himself was intended as a symbol for how all humanity should relate to him. How then, did ancient Israel understand the covenant relationship as an example for all people?

The unknown prophet who composed the second section of the book of Isaiah (Chapters 40 – 55) in the 6th century BC is perhaps the first of the great writers of Israel to show a consistent concern with the way in which Israel's destiny affects the whole human world:

> I, the Lord, have called you with righteous purpose
> and taken you by the hand;
> I have formed you, and appointed you
> to be a light to all peoples,
> a beacon for the nations.
> (Isa. 42: 6)

The phrase translated in the New English Bible, as a 'light to all peoples' can also be rendered, as in some older versions, 'a *covenant* to all peoples'. This is a rather odd expression, and 'light' may after all be the best rendering, but the idea of *Israel itself* as a sign of God's promise to all the human family is a powerful one, which does in fact capture an important element of the prophet's thinking. Israel shows to the world a model of how God involves himself in the history, and way of life, of one particular human community. So Israel reveals both a God who draws close to his world, and a humanity able to be transformed by this closeness. The presence of Israel in the world is thus a blessing for all nations (as promised to Abraham in Genesis 22: 18). It sets a standard of human wholeness, and so speaks of hope in a world of *un*wholeness: a world of slavery, idolatry and ignorance.

Bear in mind that part of Israel's history was that it was overrun by an invading army, and the people were taken captive as slaves to Babylon. With this in mind, read Jeremiah 3: 31 – 34 and Ezekiel 34: 11 – 31. Jeremiah and Ezekiel are responding to the challenge posed by the disappearance of Israel as a political entity: where *now* is the effective reality of the covenant? It has been shattered by human disloyalty, the proud human rejection of real *shalom*. God is still loyal, but how is *his* loyalty to enter the human world as something transforming, creative of common life?

The answer suggested is in terms of the law itself becoming, in a deeper sense, something that is part of human existence. The divine order and the divine peace will no longer be ideals 'out there' to which men and women must conform; God's peace and wisdom and righteousness will become the inner wellspring of people's life together, and the 'knowledge of God' will show itself in instinctively harmonious action. There will be no need for command and instruction. You can see this, if you like, as a recognition that there is no transformation of public life without inner conversion; but there is no suggestion of an either/or, a preferred order of priorities; God will act afresh to make a righteous community for himself. His action, his 'writing of the law in human hearts' will make itself visible only in the everyday reality of just action, in the way that the covenant requires.

This implies a new intimacy, a new directness, in God's relationship with his people. Ezekiel 34 paints a vivid picture of God himself setting out as a shepherd to gather his scattered flock again. The 'shepherds' of Israel, (priests, prophets and rulers) have allowed destructive forces to break God's covenant of peace in the community; now God must sweep away these human authorities and deal directly with the people. It is he, and he alone, who will unite and sustain Israel once again, and by his new covenant of *shalom* (Ezekiel 34: 25) will restore both the natural order and the political order.

So the hope for a new 'covenant' is hope for peace and integrity rooted in renewed human nature, nourished by a direct indwelling of God's spirit. It involves some kind of decisive breaking-down of the defences we erect against God (including human authority) because these contribute to the undermining of God's peace.

3.3. THE NEW COVENANT

The prophets had looked forward to the day when a restored Israel would become the magnetic focus for a new humanity: the early Church announced that this had already happened.

For the great prophets of the Old Testament, especially 'second Isaiah' and Jeremiah, the renewal of the covenant was possible only when all the false ideas about the covenant relationship had been broken by the tragedies of real human history. The lesson had to be learned that the covenant and the law were not necessarily a protection from the events of the world: what God offered was a pattern of faithful living and fellowship with himself—not success or safety.

Thus the covenant cannot enter its new and deeper phase within us without some decisive event which claims our total trust. The prophets point to this event as a hope, but never assert it as an accomplished fact. The New Testament claims that this sort of crisis has at last occurred: God has acted to break through our resistance.

For the early Christian communities, the life, death and resurrection of Jesus of Nazareth represented both God's honouring of his age-old commitment to Israel, and a new and more explicit kind of commitment on God's part to the whole world. In Jesus, Israel had been restored and renewed, and because of him the covenant relationship was open to all men and women. Jesus then, is the place where the new covenant began. Of all the New Testament writers, it is probably the author of the Letter to the Hebrews who most clearly sets out this idea. Jesus has given his whole life in faithfulness and obedience to the God of the covenant (Chapters 2 and 5). In him, God's loyalty and human loyalty are at last made one.

The life and death of Jesus meant that at last God's faithfulness and human faithfulness had been united: in one life the gift and the response are realised together. And because this human response is not just an accident (God does not hang around waiting for someone to be remarkably good before he can act), the early Christians spoke of Jesus' life as itself an act of God. Without taking away the real humanity of Jesus, God acts *in* him, taking the initiative in creating a new humanity that is capable of deeper intimacy with him. Jesus' life of total obedience does not save him from death. On the contrary, it is his obedience which makes death inevitable. The meaning of the covenant has to be spelled out in a refusal to run away from conflict, and in a refusal to engage in conflict on the terms of the aggressor: Jesus' acceptance of his death 'seals' his identity as the one who brings the covenant relationship to perfection. Faithfulness did not mean safety or 'success' for Jesus, and it will not mean safety or success for his followers either.

In the tradition associated with the Lord's Supper (Mark 14: 24; Matt. 26: 28; Luke 22: 20—in some manuscripts—and 1 Cor. 11: 25) Jesus was recalled as saying that his blood was the seal of the new covenant. In other words, almost as far back as we can go in the New Testament period, the theme of the crucifixion as the decisive crisis bringing the new age to birth is to be found. The Old Testament looked to a deliverance from external social bondage as the source of its theology: the New Testament suggests that there is a deeper bondage to be overcome—slavery to the idea that God will give an easy comfort or security. The new and fuller liberation is from the *inner* slavery to fear and self-protection, which is in fact at the heart of all *external* slaveries. As with the Israelites, God's gift to us as individuals and as the whole Church is not to be 'hoarded'. The new covenant 'written in our hearts' is the power given to us in order to create *shalom* in the external world.

3.4. PROMISE AND FULFILMENT

The Old Testament never allows us, for very long, to lose sight of the fact that its perspective is as wide as the whole of creation. Only within this perspective can we understand what ideas were available to the early Christian believers in their efforts to interpret the impact upon them of Jesus. It is not that some mysterious new 'Christian doctrine' takes over from the insights of the old Israel, nor that an individual and spiritual 'Christian message' wipes out the social concerns of the law and the prophets. The first believers simply took the bold step of saying that what had been expected or hoped for had now actually happened—hence the importance throughout so much of the New Testament of the conviction that 'the scriptures have been fulfilled'.

The good news still has to reach out to all creation, and it promises not a final devastating victory for the righteous, but the opportunity for *all* to be drawn into God's righteousness—right relation and peace. In other words, the Church has, from the start, a strong conviction that human history is a *single* drama. God's purpose is always for the whole human family. Jesus is to be, for all times and all places, the sign of God's unfailing covenant of love, the *Yes* to God's promises.

The Christian Church works on the assumption that the final boundaries are not yet drawn, and that no living person's rejection of grace or disobedience to God is irrevocable. As Paul says in the ecstatic conclusion of Romans 11, only God's gift and calling are irrevocable (11: 29). The Christian hope is the same as the hope of the great prophets—the universal community of *shalom* and justice. What is new is the deeper anchorage of that hope in the conviction that God has fulfilled his promise to take his law and his wisdom into the hearts of all human beings.

This is the ultimate assurance that God's acceptance of women and men does not rest on the uncertainties of the survival of a single nation, or a single political system. It is grounded in his gift of himself, in his Word, in the whole story of Jesus. There are thus no worldly limits to the promise. The Church cannot stop the historical process and say, '*Now* we know who's in and who's out, who's lost and who's saved', because that would be to claim a power which is God's alone.

Summary

Ancient Israel's trust in God was part of the covenant relationship. That covenant was not for Israel alone, but was a sign for the whole world. The prophets saw that something 'extra' was needed in order to draw the whole world to God, and in the New Testament we discover that this has been accomplished in the life, death and resurrection of Jesus. Thus the Christian Church has become the sign of the new covenant for the whole of humanity, and as such must strive to create *shalom* in the world.

Further study

(a) The universal covenant. Israel had its problems in sorting out how it should look at other nations. Apart from the early material in Joshua, Judges, 1 Samuel, etc., attitudes of harsh exclusiveness survive (indeed, they are deliberately revived and sharpened) in the period after the return from exile, when the Temple was being rebuilt—see Ezra 9 and 10, and Nehemiah 13: 23–31 on marriage laws designed to preserve the purity of the covenant people. It is important to grasp why the reformers of this period took so strong a line, in their fear that the demands of the covenant would be weakened. But there were those at the time who disagreed. Try reading these passages alongside the book of Ruth (which probably comes from this period) to see the response of those who believed the covenant people should welcome strangers from 'the nations'.

(b) The new covenant. Hebrews 8 and 9 is worth studying as a fairly sustained meditation on how the death of Jesus accomplishes what the old order only promises. Romans 9 – 11, difficult though it is, shows St Paul refusing to envisage an absolute breach between old and new: God acts through the world's rejection of Jesus to achieve a more total and comprehensive reconciliation. Understanding passages like these should help us to avoid that vicious distortion of Christianity which sets it apart from 'legalistic' Judaism and regards the continuing existence of Judaism as an anomaly. In a sense the debate between Christians and Jews turns not on who are the 'real' heirs of the promises, but whether it is the suffering Jewish people as a whole or the single figure of Jesus that stands as a witness to the eternal fidelity of God and the eternal validity of his calling—about which Jews and Christians agree. This might be the moment to give some more general thought to what's involved in being 'chosen' by God in the scriptural tradition.

(c) **Resurrection and community**. The first two chapters of the Acts of the Apostles carry us dramatically through the movement from resurrection and ascension to the giving of the Spirit and the formation of a community aiming at equality and justice. No doubt this is a much simplified and idealised narrative, but it might be a starting-point for looking at our own views of the connection—if any!—between the resurrection appearances and the formation of the Church (many people are still inclined to see the resurrection as a bit of an afterthought to the Cross). What risks do you think might be involved in separating what is 'done' on the Cross from the gathering together of a community of believers?

CHAPTER 4

Peace and prayer

4.1. INTRODUCTION

We saw in Chapter 1 that Israel, as a community of faith, realised that it needed to work at its own internal cohesion in order to be secure—and in order to *feel* that it was secure. The people discovered that their security, and their identity as a people, were bound up with their relationship with each other, with their neighbours, and with God. We saw how crucial it was for them to be in *right relationship* with all three—with God via a covenant of faithfulness, and with their neighbours and each other by working to create *shalom*.

In Chapter 3 we saw something of what trusting in the Lord meant for Israel as a people, and what this means for the Church as the people of God. But what is true for the community is true for each of its members: thus what is true for Israel was true for each Israelite, and what is true for the Church as a community of faith is true for each Christian. Thomas Merton, the monk who wrote so eloquently about peace says,

> 'He who attempts to act or do things for others or for the world without deepening his own self-understanding, freedom, integrity and capacity to love, will not have anything to give others. He will communicate to them nothing but the contagion of his own obsessions, his aggressions, his ego-centred ambitions, his delusions about ends and means, his doctrinaire prejudices and ideas.'
>
> (Thomas Merton, *Contemplation in a World of Action*, Unwin Paperbacks 1980, p. 164.)

It is for these reasons, as Merton spells them out, that we want to say something in this chapter about the personal processes which enable us to be more secure and confident, which enable us to be surer of our own identity because we are more firmly rooted in God. Of course, the more firmly we are rooted in God, the more open we are able to be to our own inner selves, and to others.

This process of growing towards God, inwards to our deepest selves and outwards to other people, is given many names—prayer, meditation, spirituality, the inner journey, personal integration, individuation. We shall first look at the nature of the process, and then at some of the things it involves.

4.2. LIFE AND PRAYER

Prayer, in all the traditional forms in which we think of it (confession, petition, praise and thanksgiving, contemplation) is an opportunity for gathering together our desires and commitments, letting them come further towards the light, giving them time and space to focus themselves further—and opening up the whole process a bit more to the truthfulness of God. Without the opportunity for prayer, our commitments and priorities become confused and disordered. We may start turning our enthusiasms or pet projects into rigid programmes of action or behaviour, which we then expect others to fall in line with. We can end up defending these, and ourselves, harshly and unthinkingly. We lose our ability to see ourselves and others in perspective, with humility, humour, honesty and charity.

We need to retain a sense that what we desire (for ourselves, for our family and friends, for the world) can only be provisional—'for the time being'—until we can see more clearly in the light of love what God's purposes may be. Similarly, we must remember that our understanding of ourselves, others and the world, is only partial, and that we always need to seek greater depths of understanding from our prayer and our attempts to be obedient to what God wills for us:

> Now we see only puzzling reflections
> in a mirror. . .
> My knowledge now is partial. . . .
> (1 Cor. 13: 12)

If we lose this sense of our knowledge being partial and provisional, then we begin to lose God. As we saw in Chapter 2 (see 'Peace with God' in Section 2.6), we cannot separate 'knowing God' from the daily business of living in the world and working to create *shalom.*

So prayer, which interrupts our surface preoccupations and draws us to deeper levels of attention and concern, is the point at which we get in touch again with the true nature of what lives in us—the movement begun by the creative act of God and drawn forward by the attraction of his love. If this is so, prayer needs all the components conventionally associated with it, as listed at the start of this section.

4.3. PRAYER AS OPENNESS TO OURSELVES

Prayer must involve *openness to ourselves*, the willingness to see the confusions of our motives, the ways in which our fear and defensiveness have caused, or are causing, injury. It will mean a steady attention to our incompleteness, a steady refusal to believe that we've 'made it', that we've miraculously thrown off all the fetters of our insecurity. We have to be ready to be shown (by others, or by God in the silent honesty of self-appraisal) how subtle and elusive the tricks of the frightened 'false self' can be. The 'false self' is that part of us which is self-seeking, which is a stranger to God. It is the self of the hard heart and the closed mind. It is the self of false sentiment, prey to fear and anxiety. In short, it is the 'false self' which makes God into an 'enemy'.

When, in our prayer or in our life, we discover the 'false self' at work, undermining the foundations of our love and integrity, we have to be ready not to panic, not to give way to despair or self-disgust, but to *leave it where it is*, in the light of God. We must resolve to go forward, not forgetting it, but trusting that the light which has made us see it clearly has in fact taken us a bit further forward—trusting, in other words, that *grace* is at work in this process. Not forgetting, but *accepting forgiveness* is what matters: a forgiveness which is creative of new potential.

This prayer demands that we create within ourselves a place of stillness; beyond the reading of books, even the Bible; beyond the saying of words or the thinking of thoughts, no matter how holy; a place in which we can take leave for a time from the surface preoccupations of life, and in which we may give attention to the deep aspirations normally buried under the daily round of busy activities.

This place is the silence in which we come home to ourselves, where we also come home to God; for there at the centre of our being is the place where we can encounter the God of love—ever present, ever available, ever attentive. Here, there is no place for masks, no place for pretence, no place for even false modesty. Here at the core of life there is only place for truth and honesty. Here we can confront our own evil, for evil is part of all of us: we can call it by its name and allow God to transform it. Here also we can confront our own goodness, our own gifts, our own deep aspirations, and allow them to grow and develop.

Paradoxically we hide as much from our goodness as we do from our evil. Acknowledging them both is a healing process, slowly making us whole. This is a journey of self-discovery, which is joyful and exciting, as well as sometimes being painful.

4.4. PRAYER AS OPENNESS TO GOD

Prayer must involve *openness to the gifts of God*. Thanksgiving is not a question of writing 'duty letters' to the Almighty, acknowledging presents we're not sure we want! It is, rather, an attitude of mind—an approach to the world and to life which sees all things, all people, all events as gifts from God. It is we who choose to use these gifts for good or for ill, or to ignore them. To live life treating all things as gifts—even pain and misfortune—is the deepest way of giving praise and thanks to God. We can learn from misfortune, we can grow through pain, we can delight in pleasure—all are gifts from God, if we open ourselves to them.

Thanksgiving, therefore, is the readiness to look back on events and encounters with an eye for what has challenged or enriched us—and to look around expectantly now for the same enrichment. This means a high degree of willingness to be patient with people and circumstances—patient, not in the sense of being resigned and inactive, but in tackling difficulties, bearing with tensions, in the hope that there, too, grace is to be found if we have the strength not to run away. It also means looking *affirmatively* at our own experience, developing a deeper trust of ourselves, a greater ability to express our views and needs: if God is working *through* who we are, then (imperfect and awkward as we may be) we have no call to apologise for ourselves. If we are unable to affirm ourselves, to accept ourselves, and to express our needs, then we start to slip towards a state of resenting our imperfections and our weaknesses. As we shall see later (Chapter 6), this sets us on the road of seeking and creating enemies outside ourselves, as an escape from the enemies within.

Prayer must also involve *openness to God*—not only to his 'gifts'. We have seen how the coming of God questions all our assumptions about him and what his presence means. He is not to be limited by our expectations of what he will give, and sometimes he is so far from our expectations that we cannot understand what it means for him to be 'there' at all. All prayer ultimately presses towards silence—not only the absence of words, but the putting away of images and ideas of God: waiting in what can sometimes be a deeply painful emptiness, knowing nothing but our own continuing decision to look for the *truth*. This is the prayer into which adoration and contemplation draw us: the prayer of sheer trust in God, not in any of our ideas about the world and about him. In this prayer, we take the risk of placing our security in God alone, as we *experience* him. We move beyond what we have been told about God, beyond what we think we should believe or experience, and into a new country of prayer. In one sense this is the most secure of prayers, because it leaves behind all trivial and worldly substitutes for God. In another, it is the least secure, because it leaves us with no adequate word or picture for what we encounter. But if we Christians are to talk about peace and security at all, this fundamental experience of our smallness, weakness and poverty must be at the heart of what we say and do.

4.5. PRAYER AS OPENNESS TO THE WORLD

Prayer must involve *openness to the world*. Our petitions or intercessions are one of the great tests of our commitment to peace, because such prayer demands of us a real concern to see the world from the perspective of the needs, hopes and fears of others. Being open to the world means letting ourselves be touched by the pain, the injustice, the sickness, the poverty which are suffered by others. We are part of the world, and nothing in the world is foreign to God's love, and therefore nothing in the world can be foreign to our love, if we are to be truly open to it.

To be open to the world, and to pray for peace, are not just large abstract concerns to be listed in our prayers. When we visit someone in hospital, we open ourselves to all the sickness in the world, and that is prayer. When we give time or money to help others in impoverished circumstances, we open ourselves to all the poverty in the world, and that is prayer. When, for instance, we respond to a request from Amnesty International and send a greetings card to a prisoner of conscience, we open ourselves to all the injustice in the world, and that is prayer.

It was also an act of prayer when an old-age pensioner moved into a deeply divided community in Northern Ireland, to be there and to listen to the voices of the paramilitary groups, to the hatreds and angers. (See *Time to Choose* by M. K. Barker, Alan Kreider, etc., Celebration Services (Post Green) 1979, p.79.) It is also an act of prayer to refuse to obey laws which forbid inter-racial meeting and worship. It could be an act of prayer to write a letter to a church in Eastern Europe, or the United States! (see *Beginning Now, Part 2—Peacemaking in Practice*, Chapter 6).

Again, it is an act of prayer, of openness to the world, to start a conversation with a peace-campaigner, or with a soldier (the finest prayer being to do whichever of those is the harder for you). For those concerned for peace it is essential that peace is not sought in a spirit of hatred for those who are seen as 'enemies of peace'. To pray with understanding for those caught in the insane complexities of international struggles for security and prestige is part of what's involved in acknowledging that *shalom* begins here and now, with ourselves—and that it does *not* begin with furious contempt for those we are confronting. Intercession can, and should be, a barrier-breaking activity: between nations and ideologies, between clashing groups within a society. It is a testimony to the universality of the Kingdom.

* * * * *

This chapter has no 'questions for discussion', as talking about prayer is no substitute for praying! It would be good if the time which would otherwise be spent in discussion were, for this chapter, spent in prayer.

Further study

1. Monica Furlong	*Contemplating Now*	(Hodder and Stoughton 1971)
2. Henri J. M. Nouwen	*Reaching Out*	(Collins 1976)
3. J. Neville Ward	*The Use of Praying*	(Epworth 1967)
4. Anthony de Mello	*Sadhana: A Way to God*	(published in India, but in English, in 1978. If not available from your local bookseller, copies may be obtained from: Bob Balkan, Redemptorist Publications, Alphonsus House, Chawton, Alton, Hampshire, GU34 3HQ. Tel: 0420 88222)

A list of books on prayer could be very long indeed! The above four represent a selection which cover the issues raised in this chapter. The first three are basically books *about* prayer whilst the fourth one is more of a 'how-to' book. It contains suggestions, exercises of the imagination, breathing exercises, and so on, to help the reader to learn how to pray and meditate.

CHAPTER 5

Power and conflict

5.1. INTRODUCTION

The aim of this chapter is to look at the two fundamental political problems which lie behind a lot of what we have been considering so far in this book. These two issues are *power* and *conflict*.

To start with, it may help to think about the following:

> Can you imagine a society in which there is no exercise of force? If so, what would it be like? How would it maintain internal order? How would it deal with attack from outside?
>
> If you cannot imagine such a society, are you implying that some use of force is inevitable if society is to exist at all? How much force is legitimate? Who decides? Who exercises that force? How is that force restrained within agreed limits? Can those limits be changed? How, and by whom?
>
> Is force always hostile to the vision of God's kingdom? Is it always a bad thing to precipitate conflict? If you think it is, why? If you think it isn't necessarily a bad thing, can you think of an example to show when it might be a good thing to be instrumental in bringing about open conflict?
>
> Is causing conflict always the opposite of 'reconciliation'? What can we learn from situations of conflict? How can we grow through such situations? How can conflict be limited so that it does not disrupt a community or a society completely?

This chapter will explore these issues in the context of the questions raised so far in this book. We have been suggesting that the Christian faith involves a vision of humanity capable of creative response to God's call and God's faithfulness. Christianity does not regard that human capability as something that comes about only by divine action. The initiative is always God's, but our response is in the trial and error of everyday life in the human community. It is there that the nature and scope of a God-directed humanity must be discovered and made real.

5.2. COMMUNITY AND COERCION

If you think about it, it is rather odd that people have ever thought that harmony or justice could come into being entirely spontaneously in human groups. We have said enough about the ways in which our fear and insecurity 'freeze' into defensive–aggressive postures; no collection of human beings begins with a clean slate. We take it for granted that in communities aiming at some kind of balance and long-term coherence there are—at the very least—conventions about acceptable and unacceptable behaviour in ways of relating to one another, and sanctions for defending these conventions. At the most basic level, games have rules, languages have grammar. To communicate at all, to live or act intelligently, alongside others, there must be a common medium of exchange, an agreed common ground of some sort and thus, too, some way of identifying 'mistakes' or false or disruptive moves. And if a person doesn't see the nature of their mistake, the result is that they are no longer sharing in the same activity or language or style of life, and steps may be taken to exclude them, to the extent that they make it impossible for other members of the group to pursue their agreed goals.

> As an example of the very real presence of these rules, try reflecting on the ways in which we teach children to say 'please' and 'thank you', to speak 'properly' and so on. What are the sanctions we employ, both as individual adults and as a society, against children who fail to learn the rules or refuse to conform to them?

St Thomas Aquinas (1225–74) defined 'violence' as anything which restricts a person's power to do what they want, and in this sense it is clear that any and every coherent human association may find itself practising violence. But the point is that it is exercised to prevent a person or subgroup affecting the liberty of the group *as a whole* to do what *it* has chosen to do. The initial 'violence', you could say, comes from the minority of dissidents who are attacking what this group has as a matter of fact set out to do.

> Consider the following example: in a small town there is an area of rough wooded ground where people like to walk their dogs, and where children play. In the course of planning a new traffic scheme for the area, the authorities decide to build a road across this piece of land. The residents protest in the usual way, with petitions and so forth, but to no avail. The scheme goes ahead. On the day when the first bulldozers arrive, a group of residents sit down in the road to block access to the land. The police are called to remove the protesters, one of whom is accidentally injured. This angers another, who retaliates, and a fight breaks out between the

police and the residents. One policeman is injured and one resident is charged with assaulting a police officer.

Now, taking Aquinas' definition of 'violence' given above, where did the violence in this situation originate? Was it in the authorities who tried to stop a group of residents doing what they wanted to do? Was it in the residents trying to stop a legally constituted authority doing what it wanted to do? Was it in the people who sat in the road? Or in the people who called the police? Or in the driver of the bulldozer? Or in the police officers? Or is the violence, in Aquinas' sense of the word, part and parcel of a society in which certain groups of people are elected or appointed to take decisions on behalf of the rest of us?

Notice what Aquinas' definition takes for granted:

(i) you have a group of people who are pretty clear about what they have come together to do;
(ii) there are some agreed conventions for recognising what does and what doesn't count as a move towards these agreed aims;
(iii) the dissident doesn't succeed in convincing the group (or whoever speaks for the group) that what he or she wants, or the way he or she wants to pursue the agreed goals, is actually compatible with the way most of the group have understood what they're after;
(iv) anyone joining a common project or activity relinquishes their absolute power to do what they want: there is a (spoken or unspoken) element of *contract* involved.

In this kind of setting, coercion is practised *for the sake of liberty of the majority*; or, in slightly different terms, power is exercised to guarantee the power of members of a group to do what they have (jointly) agreed and decided to do. This sort of analysis works quite well with a variety of small-scale groups and clearly defined activities. If someone picks up the ball in a football match, starts playing a tuba in a string-quartet, or (more disastrously) drives on the wrong side of the road, we have simple ways of identifying what's wrong and taking appropriate restraining action. It works too, though less clearly, at the rather more complex level of groups bound together by wider projects and commitments—religious or political associations. If there is less clarity in these contexts, it is often because religious and political bodies are by their nature bound to spend some of their energy in responding to rapidly changing circumstances. Should Christian doctors perform abortions? How much political activism outside Parliament is consistent with membership of the Labour Party? These, and similar, issues obviously cannot be settled by an appeal to some clearly laid down set of rules for behaviour.

However, the basic structures are still the same. The uncertainty arises largely because the debate about compatibility (number (iii) in the list above of things taken for granted) is still in full swing. Presumably there is no dissident or innovator in groups like those mentioned who would suggest that absolutely anything is acceptable behaviour for members of those groups. So there are some agreed rules.

We have stressed in Chapter 3 that the body of Christian believers sets out to be comprehensive, non-exclusive, and so on. What this means is that no one who *wants* to make a commitment to this way of life and belief is automatically ruled out by accident of race, class, intelligence, or whatever. However, it remains true that choices involve renunciation. To choose to do one thing is to choose not to do another, and to join the Christian body is to make certain choices. To join with reservations, deliberately hanging on to alien attitudes of self-interest, sectarianism, self-gratification, deep mistrust, etc., is to invite criticism, discipline and perhaps expulsion. If people deceive themselves about the compatibility of their faith with certain social attitudes, or with certain personal or group practices, then the church has a responsibility to undeceive them.

Bonhoeffer put it this way:

> 'For the church to deny its boundaries is no work of mercy. The true church comes up against boundaries. In recognising them it does the work of love towards men by honouring the truth.'
>
> (Dietrich Bonhoeffer, *The Way to Freedom*, Fontana 1972, p. 95.)

He was commenting in 1936 on the status of the 'Confessing Church', which had set itself up in opposition to the German state churches on the grounds that these churches were subservient to Hitler's regime.

So the process is still in principle fairly straightforward. Communities defined by a purpose are, of their very nature, bound to exercise coercion of some sort in securing their own freedom to do what they have decided to do. But what about the human groupings we don't *decide* to join, and which aren't obviously defined by specific goals? We do not really have any option about belonging to 'society', being a citizen in a particular state. How then do power and coercion work in this context?

The simple answer is that coercive power is exercised so that a society or state may *survive*. What is ruled out as unlawful, and liable to sanctions, is what imperils the general stability of this system of administration (law, commerce and finance, public planning, defence and security, etc.). If we ask what makes law 'lawful' or justice 'just', the answer will be given in terms of what will keep the system working.

This is not a bad answer, as far as it goes, but it is in danger of becoming rather disturbingly circular if left as it stands. It tends to assume that this particular system is good by definition: what is good for it must be automatically just, what is bad for it automatically unlawful. This is why so many discussions at international level about human rights so rarely produce a constructive outcome. In one system, a degree of individual liberty helps that system to continue to function well. In another system, only a high degree of conformity, enforced as necessary, will enable that system to continue. To bring questions of morality and the rights of individuals into the debate is to take the discussion into new territory which is not recognised by one of the parties involved.

There is another danger, though, in defining as 'just' what is good for society in its present condition. No system remains absolutely the same for an indefinite length of time, so there is a risk of it slowly, and even unconsciously, changing its actual standards of justice and equity. These changes may be in response to internal or external pressures on security, to unrest at home or abroad. In other words, democratic states may slip slowly towards tyranny if they lack a clear aim other than mere control and self-perpetuation.

In practice, societies normally justify their legal coercion by some kind of appeal to the common good or the welfare of the majority. There are two possible ways of understanding this, however. A government may use this language in an implicitly authoritarian way, by assuming that it is the agents of government who have the exclusive and undisputed right to define 'good' and 'welfare'. In this case we are back with the problem outlined above, of how this can be prevented from turning into control for the sake of control. Alternatively, the appeal to the common good may be an invitation to some kind of public debate about the nature of social health (an aspect, remember, of *shalom*). This is an admission that the government concerned is accountable to the people.

In the first case, government exists to determine and impose programmes. In the second, it exists to interpret a consensus in society.

In the second case, society at large is seen as being at least a bit more like a voluntary and purposive body; it is organised so as to allow people to ask, 'What for?' about policy and practice. Coercion is justified on the grounds that the existing power structures can be shown to rest on a real measure of consent. This in turn assumes that the workings of government are open to inspection, even if only in the rather reduced sense that governments have to explain themselves to electorates at regular intervals—and ideally in a much fuller way, including, for instance, *some* right of access to personal files for those likely to be affected by use of the information they contain.

When 'the rule of law' appears to be breaking down in a society, in the sense that the legal process is widely flouted or bypassed, it is not safe just to assume that a wave of simple criminal energy is sweeping the population. It is more likely that there is (whether for good reason or not) a widespread feeling that lawmaking and decision-making no longer rest on a true consensus, that the debate on social health has been cut short. In such circumstances, people are regularly driven to ask more searching questions than hitherto about justice and welfare, and about what the administration of society is, in the long run, answerable to. These are the circumstances in which important confrontations occur, clarifying people's vision, and forcing decisions about values. This process can often liberate citizens from an unthinking assumption that the administration knows best and can always be relied on for acceptable definitions of the good and the just.

Summary

So it seems that in society at large it can be true, as it is for smaller groups, that *legitimate* power and force depend upon the possibility of showing that they are exercised for the *empowering* of a majority to pursue goals that have been debated and agreed.

For discussion

Can you think of one modern-day example of a government using legitimate power and force, in the sense summmarised above? What is the evidence that the goals were widely agreed?

Can you think of an example when such force was not legitimate in the above sense? i.e. that the goals clearly had not been publicly debated—or, if debated, were not agreed.

5.3. THE IMPORTANCE OF CONFLICT

What we have just said takes it for granted that, in fact, vigorous social life will very seldom be 'peaceful' in the 'peace and quiet' sense of the word. Living communities of any kind are bound to be struggling for equilibrium as cultural and technological development pose new problems. Can full employment survive the arrival of microchip technology and similar advances in the information sciences? If not, what will full participation in the productive life of society actually mean for a skilled worker in thirty years' time? Questions like these should raise very acutely what 'justice' and 'welfare' involve—and ultimately what 'human fulfilment' means. These are all questions about *shalom*. Our present tragedy in the 'de-industrialising' nations is that these issues are largely avoided. However, this is precisely the sort of setting in which some groups within society, with a commitment to particular visions of humanity, can emerge to stimulate debate. By virtue of their commitment they can challenge the state, in effect, to *take sides*, after a process of public discussion, on the question of what is good for people. The Church is, of course, one such group.

This 'debate' may sound rather intellectualist—just an exchange of ideas. But there are other issues where debate is only generated at any serious level by conscientious, carefully planned action, i.e. by provoking *conflict.* As we saw above, it is often only when social protest puts into question the reality of 'consensus' that people are driven to look at their presuppositions—the first requirement of worthwhile debate. We would want to stress the words 'conscientious, carefully planned action', though: there are appallingly sterile conflicts between groups, or between the state and protesting bodies, when action is thoughtlessly provocative of nothing more than angry retaliation. Useful confrontation has to draw out from the other side some kind of justification for actions and policies which have not yet been properly and publicly examined.

For discussion

Some years ago Friends of the Earth mounted a campaign to return thousands of 'disposable' soft-drink bottles to the headquarters of the firm which manufactured them. This stimulated a lot of public debate at the time about our 'throw-away' society. The firm concerned still makes disposable bottles, but there has been an increase in awareness of the necessity for recycling waste products, and many towns now have 'bottle-banks'. Was this a constructive confrontation?

More recently, the activities of the Campaign for Nuclear Disarmament and of the women campers at Greenham Common have brought the issues of nuclear weapons to the attention of the general public. The campaigners have been in very direct conflict with the government, in terms of ideas, and with the police in face-to-face confrontation. The government has responded with public information about its defence policies, particularly in relation to nuclear weapons, and has entered the public debate to justify its policies. Does this amount to a useful confrontation?

Occasionally, the immediate practical effects of 'action' will be to draw out the irrationality of the other side, and that may mean a violent response to protest. An example of this is the terrible time of the early days of the Civil Rights campaign in the American South in the early sixties. Yet the *long-term* aim of such action is still to bring issues into public visible debate. The common failing of violent protest (using 'violent' in the usual sense here, rather than in the more general way that St Thomas Aquinas suggests) is that it aims to attack outright, as if its objectives were simply to defeat an uncompromisingly hostile force. It makes the mistake of taking for granted that the *natural* relationship between a protesting body and the state is absolute opposition, so that change can only come about by the submission of the governing power. This suggests that the protesting group itself does not have much interest in the processes of public debate and accountability.

There are some situations in which such opposition really does seem to be inevitable: how much has non-violent protest really achieved in South Africa over thirty years or so? But in states where the government is still accountable, in theory, to the whole adult population, it is damaging and foolish to take up melodramatic revolutionary postures.

Conflict, whether conducted by writing, verbal dispute, 'direct action', or all of them, is simply an aspect of how our society has always kept itself alive and moving, and answerable to certain values. The abolition of the slave trade, the great Parliamentary reforms of the 19th century, votes for women—the British political tradition is not such a very 'peaceful' one. All these matters involved serious and dramatic confrontation in their day.

Christians talk very eagerly of the urgent need for reconciliation between different groupings in society, between management and unions, between black and white communities, or between black communities and the police. When the real clash between groups is so serious that we cannot speak truthfully about social consensus, or 'justice being seen to be done', there must be some of us prepared to insist on public recognition of these things, and public debate. In other words, to break the appearance of consensus in order to ask where *justice* lies: to ask whether an administration which ignores, or colludes with, deep (and deepening) divisions in society has a viable idea of what it means by the health (*shalom*) of society.

To summarise. Our main concern is to suggest that conflict and confrontation are not themselves wicked or destructive. They are seen like this generally in societies that have got used to being passive, and avoiding major discussions about shared values. They are also seen like this by governments that are nervous about public accountability—often because of some uncertainty about the reality of the consensus they claim to represent. The paradox is that the exercise of power may be more decisive and effective in the long term in societies that allow for a good deal of public debate and expression of social tension and conflict. The repression of this by authoritarian and unchallengeable power simply increases the likelihood that conflict in the long term will be a matter of violent opposition and immovable confrontation. In other words, it increases the insecurity which already underlies and prompts repression.

5.4. POWER, CONFLICT AND THE GOSPEL

Here are two plausible statements:

> 'The church is called to share the vulnerability of Christ crucified. It can have no interest in power';

'The church is called to share the reconciling work of Christ. It can have no part in generating conflict'.

Both these statements could be defended on the basis of *some* of what's been said earlier in this book. If you have followed this chapter so far it may be clear why we don't think they are the natural consequence of the argument as a whole. The Church, if it is true to itself, will have a good deal to say about vulnerability. It invites those who enter it to a life of trustfulness, acknowledging that this is anything but a guarantee of success or security in worldly terms. This means that it is a critical and *self*-critical body. As we saw at the beginning of this chapter, and in earlier sections, it has the right to 'honour the truth' by denouncing what in its own life draws it towards an idolatrous bondage to tangible securities, and challenging those members who refuse to throw off such a bondage. In doing so, it must attend to its own methods and means of exercising authority, to guard against the traps of Pharisaism and authoritarianism; i.e. it must be aware of, and interested in, *how* it exercises power. The Church must strive to live out what it preaches.

Furthermore, Christians (in spite of popular belief to the contrary) don't and can't lead divided lives, with radically different standards and hopes in their 'religious' and their 'secular' activities. The Church commends trustfulness as an ideal for *human living* not just for a ghetto within it called 'religious belief'; so, if society is administered in a way which runs counter to this ideal, nationally and internationally, then the Church can reasonably be expected to object—just as it would in a society which condoned racialism, slavery or infanticide. And in this sense too it cannot avoid being interested in power. What access does it have to the channels of public discussion? What problems underlie the insecurities of an administration? What are the insoluble tensions of public life, and what are the ones that *can* be helped?

The tempting short cut is to say, 'worldly power is a realm where there are no absolute rights and wrongs, an area of tragic compromises; the church can offer nothing but understanding and forgiveness'. There is a good deal of truth in this, but also a dangerous hint that one form of 'worldly power' is pretty much like another in moral and spiritual terms, as if no choices could be made, and as if 'visions of humanity' are necessarily very remote indeed from the realities of decision-making. The Church, as we recognised earlier, cannot expect perfection. However, to accept the inevitability of compromise doesn't remove the need to choose between the available imperfections, and to ask pretty sharply for justification of this or that *particular* compromise.

The real truth of the first statement at the start of this section is that the Church obviously has no right to speak and act as if it could dictate to the state. It must live with the fact that there are areas of legislation in which its views are unlikely to prevail. We have learned (for the most part) to live with this where divorce law is concerned. Like other groups defending a specific view of what humanity is 'about', the Church must risk itself in general debate, and rely on persuasive argument. This includes, in serious matters of human equity and human flourishing, whatever degree of critical confrontation it believes appropriate. We can remember Bonhoeffer again here.

What about reconciliation? We have already heard, in Chapter 2, Jeremiah and Ezekiel castigating those who say *shalom* where there is none. There is also a popular saying that things will get worse before they get better. How is reconciliation to be real unless conflicts have been honestly faced? In Chapter 2 we saw how it is only the proclaiming and offering of God's peace which shows us our own illusions about peace. Likewise in this connection, if there are real conflicts and problems beneath the surface of society, the Church's calling may at times be to provoke a more open acknowledgement of the conflict. Otherwise the good news of reconciliation becomes a cheap reassurance—dressing the wounds only skin-deep, as Jeremiah puts it.

We have assumed throughout that the Church's responsibility for preaching the Gospel to the world is primarily to *be itself*; but secondarily its responsibility is to *be itself in and among* the debates that are essential to a creative society. If a sane society is one which nourishes debate, it should be one which expects criticism as well as support from the Church. If it expects the Church to play a conciliatory role quite unconnected with choosing or evaluating possible courses of action, then it has misunderstood the nature of the whole of the Christian tradition. To say this is no daring innovation: it would be quite hard to find any major writer of the Christian past denying all rights of criticism to the Church—though there is plenty of disagreement about how actively and openly this criticism should be expressed.

The truth of the second statement given earlier is that the Church's theology asserts that any oppositions or conflicts between people are, in the end, resolvable. This is not bland optimism: as a mere matter of fact, it is obvious that plenty of conflicts *don't* get resolved; but to assume that they *can't* be resolved is to assume that history is farce, that change is unthinkable, and that half the world is naturally good and the rest bad. Trying to reconcile *that* with the Gospel of Jesus is a lost cause.

In taking a critical stance, the churches may draw out some painful polarisations, especially in the area of reflecting on peace, internal and external. This is because they believe that the one central thing which makes *shalom* more and more remote is the corrupting idea that there are certain kinds of conflict that are more or less eternal and necessary. The Church affirms that what is eternal and necessary is God—his will and his peace alone. Conflict is important, but it is important as a sign of life and growth, not as an end in itself. In *that* sense, the Church must preach reconciliation above everything else—the reconciliation which is the ultimate harmony in creation, and between God and creation, on which all things rest, and to which we hope and pray all things will move; nothing less final than that. What the Church is at war with is what

Bonhoeffer calls 'cheap grace'—glib, superficial and temporary conciliation.

We end this chapter with a strong statement from an American writer, on the consequences of taking 'absolute opposition' for granted. It points to what Christians ought to be confronting and battling against. It also shows what happens to real power and liberty if anxiety about conflict is projected on to an external opposite which is then seen as entirely devilish. Thus it draws together both the themes of this chapter. It also opens up the area we shall be discussing in the final chapter: the need for a hard look at the roots of aggression and enmity in our distorted and troubled inner lives, and thus the need for 'interior peacemaking'.

> 'The worst in communism—the readiness to resort to any means and to sacrifice any number of people in what is proclaimed as the public interest—has come to dominate the national posture of the United States. And communist countries have fallen to the forces of reaction, for they are shaped not by their own best ideals but by reaction to Western military pressures. In the spiraling nuclear arms competition each side erodes and undermines the remaining good sense, high hopes and humaneness of the other. The vitriol that envelops both East and West etches on each side the mirror image of that which is feared and deplored in the other.'
>
> (Dale Aukerman, *Darkening Valley. A Biblical Perspective on Nuclear War*, Seabury Press 1981, distributed in Britain by SPCK.)

Further Study

(a) **The Sermon on the Mount (Matt. 5–7)**. Look especially at Matt. 7:1–5. Much of the chapter you have just read could be taken as arguing for the *passing of judgement* on society and political life. Is this compatible with the recorded words of Jesus here? Is there any way of helpfully distinguishing between not judging and apathetic indifference?

(b) **'Direct action'**. Stephen Oates' biography of Martin Luther King, *Let the Trumpet Sound* (London, Search Press 1982), will provide ample material for thinking about what is involved in planning for constructive conflict—including the risks of hysterical violence being the first response. Parts 4 and 5 deal at length with the devastating early years of King's campaign.

(c) **Conflict**. Try collecting—over a week or so—accounts of what are called 'conflicts' and 'clashes' in the press: industrial disputes, international and economic tensions, political manoeuvrings in the main parties, disagreements about educational or social planning, etc. If you follow these through in one particular newspaper, you should be in a position to assess how far the reporting and general treatment suggests a particular judgement on conflict—as a bad thing or a healthy thing—and also to tease out some of the underlying principles or even rival 'visions' that sustain these confrontations.

(d) Taking action ourselves. *Beginning Now, Part 2—Peacemaking in Practice* contains many ideas for internal and external peacemaking.

CHAPTER 6

Enemies

6.1. INTRODUCTION

In this final chapter, the aim is to bring the whole of this discussion back to ourselves as persons. Enmity, exclusion and dread in social life take root because we are all liable to these things in our individual lives; and we suffer as individuals from this emotional and spiritual deprivation partly because of the societies we live in.

Last year at a conference about the military use of the Pacific, a woman from one of the Pacific islands was describing the terrible destruction caused by atomic weapons testing in the Pacific, and then said, 'We were told it was necessary to protect us from our enemies. But we have no enemies. Our language does not even have a word for *enemy*.' This raises many questions for us, which we shall begin to examine in Section 6.2, 'Do we need enemies?'. To make an enemy of someone—or not—is a choice we make, and this section looks at some of the personal and social processes involved in creating 'enemies'.

In Section 6.3, we look at what our enemies can tell us about ourselves. We ask the question: do we make enemies that merely mirror what we most fear or dislike in ourselves?

In Section 6.4, we examine Jesus' radical solution, 'Love your enemies', and ask what that might mean in modern-day terms.

Finally, in Section 6.5, we consider 'converting the imagination'—the nature of the inner changes we must make if we are to love our enemies, and convert enmities into partnerships. This builds on the discussion of prayer in Chapter 4.

As we come to the end of this book, we see that the Gospel call to us to be peacemakers must move us from theory to practice, from discussion to action. Thus the 'Further Study' for this chapter is *Beginning Now, Part 2—Peacemaking in Practice*.

6.2. DO WE NEED ENEMIES?

Jesus instructed his followers to love their enemies; in other words, he took it for granted that we've *got* enemies. He's not talking in sweeping generalities about the people publicly designated The Enemy in times of war or stress (Germans, Russians, Argentinians) but—as the text goes on to make clear—people directly related to us whom we see as hostile: 'pray for your persecutors and those who treat you spitefully' (Matt. 5: 44). Enemies are people committed to our extermination, or at the very least our humiliation, and Jesus acknowledges that the typical human response is to carry on the battle in these terms. With someone we perceive as out for our humiliation, we are fighting for our lives.

But, says Jesus, God the creator gives equally to all. The world is not different for the good and the bad. If we are to be of God's family we must aim at the same steadiness of response. 'Be ye therefore perfect', said the older translations, avoiding the rather alarming moral precept of the New English Bible—'There must be no limit to your goodness'. 'Be perfect' is much more like 'Be singleminded' or even perhaps 'Be faithful'. Like God, do not be turned away from a just and generous vision of events and people by the presence of evil, aggression or rejection.

What makes this so hard for us? God is what he is by nature, but we have to 'make ourselves', to work towards what he designs us to be. For us the future is uncertain, and unless we have confidence in our resources to meet it, it will be a constant threat against which we must secure ourselves. But how are we to have confidence in our resources? We know ourselves to be in varying degrees cut off from our deepest human possibilities. We long for an *unconditional* affirmation which we never discover in our memories. We are marked by emotional scars buried too deeply in us to be easily understood.

Anything and anyone that reinforces this sense of our lack, or alienation, reinforces our unconfidence and thus intensifies the threatening nature of what may lie ahead. People who challenge us, who undermine things we take for granted, who dismiss us and will not take us seriously, or who actively attack us, become representatives of the general threateningness of going on living. They may have no deliberate intention of undermining us, but they do. And the more we attribute either ill-will or destructive power to them, the more we fix their image in our minds as *enemies*.

What really threaten us are our own inner divisions, our lack of direction, our uncertainty about our resources for more crises, sometimes our fear of tendencies in ourselves which might surface in a disastrous or shocking way. So the darkness in us (our suspicion, ignorance and fear of ourselves) is dramatically portrayed in the image of an 'enemy'. This is not to say, of course, that there are never people who *really* threaten our safety or survival!—a friend in a religious community once remarked, 'Brother A thinks Father B is persecuting him. Father B thinks Brother A is paranoid. The trouble is that they're both right!' The heart of the problem is our dread of them, our decision to treat them as an 'enemy', and thus the tendency to assume more and more that all they say or do is deliberately aimed at our weakness, and this is what often keeps us from honest confrontation of that very weakness.

The *advantage* of having an enemy is that we are, at one level anyway, enabled to get rid of our own inner complexities and our self-doubts. We can tell ourselves that the *real* cause of our suspicion or uncertainty about this or that memory, tendency or motivation in us is that it is under attack; the fragmentation is imposed from outside. The cracks in the wall are, so to speak, the result of enemy shelling, not of shaky foundations. Having an enemy works curiously well as a means of propping up our confidence; the world is at last neatly organised into light and dark, inside and outside. Fear of the future is rather lessened by the fact that so long as we have a means of keeping the source of our fears *outside* ourselves, we can more easily see ourselves as strong and good.

This postpones indefinitely the problems of coming to terms with our own weakness, and in the long term it also adds a further twist to our anxiety. If we need enemies outside to keep up our sense of our own worth we have to make sure that they are always available. Most people, if they are honest, will admit to 'making' others into enemies on occasions:

— the child who is (legitimately) rebuked by a teacher for misbehaviour will complain of being 'picked on', as if the teacher held a personal grudge. This is easier for the child than admitting to being in the wrong;
— someone who opposes our plans or ideas may be seen as being personally undermining;
— someone pursuing a course of action purely out of their own self interest may, if that action is inconvenient or displeasing to us, be interpreted as 'having it in for us'.

Even God is turned into an 'enemy' when, after a run of bad luck or misfortune of some kind, a person is heard to remark, 'I think God must be punishing me for something'.

We can—more or less—recognise unreasonable suspicion when we see it in individuals; we are usually rather wary of extremist groups that interpret all world events as the products of some subtle and comprehensive plot by Jews, Freemasons, the CIA, the KGB and so on; and we are *almost* equally suspicious of those who try to persuade us that extremist groups of left or right are behind any slight hiccup in the running of society. When Iranian Muslims describe the U.S.A. as 'the great Satan', we dismiss this as ignorant fanaticism. We are a bit less ready to acknowledge the extent to which we may be manipulated into seeing 'the Eastern bloc' as similarly evil; again, though, we can see something of how the Soviet Union constructs *its* conspiracy theories of world power-politics. What we need to work on is, in all such cases, *why* persons and groups need to create devils like this. It's no use simply writing it all off by shrugging our shoulders, and saying, 'People are like that'. We should be asking what it is in the history of Iran or Russia or the U.S.A., or even some peculiar and marginal political group with a passionate conviction about the 'real' causes of history, that generates such fear. To answer that requires some self-understanding. We need some grasp of the inner feelings of deprivation or exclusion from 'grace' and acceptance, that make groups, as much as individuals, set up dramatic and exclusive oppositions.

It was St Augustine, at the beginning of the 5th century, who seems to have been the first to elaborate the idea of the *need* for enemies. In the first book of his vast work *The City of God*, he goes over the early history of the ancient Roman state in order to show that, without the stimulus of an external enemy, social life in the republic slid faster and faster towards economic injustice and tyranny. When the armies of Carthage threatened from outside, Rome pulled together to fight them off; but this had the effect of concealing the lack of real coherence in the state, true peace and justice. Without the enforced unity of wartime, the deep tensions in society came to the surface, and at last could be controlled only by dictatorship. Augustine refers to the story of the one Roman statesman who had the candour to say, when Carthage was at last at the mercy of Rome, that the enemy should *not* be destroyed because the moral structure and cement of the republic would vanish without an outside threat to enforce order.

However, it is not only ancient Rome where there was apparently a need for an enemy. The same could be said to apply to modern South Africa, for instance. The Afrikaans-speaking Christians, being devout Calvinists, believed themselves to be the new Israel. In 1836 they trekked by ox-wagon away from British rule in the Cape Colony, and were attacked by the Zulu warriors as they entered their territories. In response they formed their wagons into a circle (laager) and defended themselves: their wives and children on the inside, their enemies outside. From this developed an attitude that the world was hostile to them, and so the English language acquired a word for what had become a reality for them—the 'laager mentality'. Unity would be preserved by fighting their enemies, so much so that when their internal unity was threatened they would create or provoke an enemy to distract them from their own divisions. Over the last hundred years the enemy has changed (first the English, then the Catholics, then the Blacks and now the Communists), but the process has remained the same.

South Africa provides a stark example, but is not a similar process at work in other societies, our own included? The name of the enemy changes, but our attitudes remain remarkably fixed.

Augustine is arguing, in the whole of *The City of God*, that only the believing community has real *internal* unity, with no need for outside enemies. The 'City of God' is thus a continuing challenge to the 'earthly city', and its false security. The Church should not be interesed in fighting, or evading persecution: it will have to endure assault and work through it, but it is not permitted to hate its persecutors. 'Enemies' they most certainly are, in an objective sense, but for the Church they cannot simply be labelled and left like that. The Church's responsibility to them is unchanged.

Part of this responsibility is to go on exposing that central core of weakness in the human spirit which continues to hold on to our enemies at all costs. It is what Augustine speaks of elsewhere (in the *Confessions*) as the refusal to be 'at home' with ourselves, to look for God in the depths of ourselves. Our weakness drives us out, away from our centre. It makes us look for satisfaction and securities in worldly comfort or success. It gives us huge and unrealistic emotional expectations of our relationships. It makes us defend ourselves against evil by making evil an identifiable 'thing'. All of this is part of the process whereby we create and maintain our reassuring enemies, and take refuge in the 'earthly city' of high walls and closed gates, exclusion and repression. The Church's calling is to show that another kind of 'city' can exist—imperfectly, awkwardly and shakily, but still visibly. There *is* another possible response to our inner lack, our mistrust of ourselves and so of all others. The gospel will tell us (if we let it) that, after all, we do *not* need enemies if we are to live in this world.

6.3. THE MIRROR IMAGE OF OURSELVES

Read again the quotation from Dale Aukerman at the end of the last chapter. He points out that the Soviet Union and the United States, locked together as 'enemies', mirror each other in attitudes and behaviour.

During the First World War, the British and German propaganda organisations created very similar stories about each other. Each government was trying to convince its own citizens that 'the other side' was evil, brutish and somehow less than human. One such example was when each side accused the other of melting down corpses to make glycerine. Again, two enemies locked together mirror each other.

During the war in the South Atlantic it was being said in this country that the Argentine Junta only wanted a war in order to distract from economic and social problems at home—they needed an outside enemy because of domestic discontent. But were we not also suffering from economic problems? Was it not also a distraction for us to focus on an outside enemy instead of on our domestic problems? To what extent did Britain and Argentina come to mirror each other as 'enemies'?

It is harder to see the mirroring process at work when we are one of the actors in the drama. Naturally, we think that we are right and the 'enemy' is wrong. So let us return to the example of South Africa, given in the last section, to see if we can gain a better understanding of the processes that were (and still are) at work.

The Calvinist Afrikaaners saw themselves as the new Israel, struggling to retain their identity and security among alien, hostile, 'heathen' black people. It was very hard, in these circumstances, for people who regarded themselves as 'holy' to acknowledge their own aggression, weakness, failure or sin. They built on such texts as Joshua 9:21, in which an alien people, who dwell in the same land as the Israelites, are condemned to be 'hewers of wood and drawers of water', and to remain as servants. Thus the Afrikaaners thought they had found biblical justification for what they saw as their own superiority, and the inferiority of the black people.

The black people were presumed to be all the things that these white settlers presumed *themselves* not to be (or wished that they were not). So the black people were imagined to be dirty, lazy, indolent, violent, sexually menacing, incapable of rational thought, animal-like, and so on. In projecting these characteristics onto the black people, the Afrikaaners were denying them in themselves.

It is an example of that tendency in all of us which may be represented by

> I am individual,
> you are eccentric,
> they are mad.

When this projection is purely person-to-person, then it may damage one relationship and diminish two people. When projection is employed by a whole group of people on to another whole group, then dire social consequences may follow.

Because the Afrikaaners had superior military and technological power they were able to take control of the black people whose land they had usurped, and enslave them. Thus the black people, able to know very little except what the Afrikaaners permitted, came to see themselves as the white people told them they were. As they saw themselves, so they started to behave, and so the white people responded. Both black and white were involved in living out self-fulfilling prophecies. As a result, both peoples have been impoverished, and only now are they coming to terms with what this has meant, and continues to mean.

It was relatively easy for the white people to deceive themselves in the manner explained. The symbols of their faith already associated 'white' with grace, life, holiness and so on, while 'black' was associated with sin, death, the devil, etc. This does not mean, of course, that this is the only source of enmity in South Africa, nor that white South Africans are the only ones who are prejudiced, nor that, given the same circumstances, we would necessarily act differently—Rhodesia, a former British colony, was not noted for its enlightenment on racial matters.

For another example out of history, this time from further back, you might like to recall the period of witch-burning. The burning of witches was not 'spontaneous peasant behaviour', but was systematic and calculated action by the Church authorities of the day. The women were accused of sexual perversion and of having magical powers. Supposed magical powers were seen as coming from the devil, and so they were perceived as sinful, as was the alleged sexual behaviour. Thus the witch-burning can be seen as an attempt to remove sin from society—doomed to failure, of course, because sin lies within all of us, including the Church officials responsible for persecuting these women.

A more modern example of similar processes may be found in Hitler's Germany. The German economy lay in ruins, and the national pride of the people was at rock-bottom. The idea of an Aryan super-race, tall, blonde, blue-eyed and in all things pure and beautiful, was obviously powerfully attractive. As the whole German people was manifestly *not* like this, the 'solution' (Hitler's 'final solution') was to exterminate all who did not fit the ideal. First the Jews, but then also the gypsies, the homosexuals and so on. There was no end to the list of 'enemies', and there *could* be no end. The 'enemy' again, lay within each person and so no amount of exterminating external 'enemies' could produce the desired ideal purity.

So what is the root of these social phenomena described above? Einstein wrote to Freud, in 1932, that unless we come to terms with our unconscious predisposition to violence, there can be little hope of world peace. We all have to confront our own internal demons, to acknowledge our own buried (or not so buried!) aggression. And we need to become more aware of how often we, as individuals and as groups or whole societies, see in others precisely the characteristics we most dislike or fear in ourselves.

You might like to try a little experiment with yourself:

1. Think of a person you find it hard to get on with—maybe someone you find irritating, someone who makes you angry, or someone you just dislike.
2. Take a sheet of paper, and write this person's name at the top. Now write a list of the characteristics, attitudes, or behaviours of this person. List as many as you can—some may be just adjectives describing the person (as you perceive him or her), some may be phrases.
3. When you have listed everything you can think of about this person, go down the list and underline the particular characteristics that you most dislike. Then put the paper aside.
4. Now take a new sheet of paper, and write your own name at the top. Make a list of adjectives that you think describe yourself, and phrases that describe your own attitudes and behaviour.
5. When you've written all the descriptive words you can think of, go down the list and put a tick against the characteristics that you like, that you're glad you've got, the talents you've been blessed with. Then go down the list again and put a cross against the descriptions of yourself that you don't like, that you wish weren't true.

6. Now compare the crosses on your list with the characteristics you underlined on the first list. You may find there are similarities, that the aspects of the other person which you dislike are also the aspects of yourself which you dislike.

So, if we react like this as individuals, is it surprising that groups and whole societies also behave in this way?

As a postscript to this little experiment, it is worth remembering that if you make an enemy of someone, then you become that person's enemy, too. Point 6 above is a first step in converting that enmity—to recognise your own part in it. A good second step might be to return to the list of descriptions of the other person, and now to circle the characteristics of that person which you *do* like—or, if there are none of those on the list, to add some!

Our Christian tradition has encouraged us to flee from sin, but there are sinful elements in all of us—parts of ourselves that have become distorted, or which are undeveloped. Perhaps we could try to befriend these elements, acknowledge their presence within us, and allow them, under grace, to be transformed. In so doing we not only grow in maturity ourselves, but also learn to see others more clearly, accepting their gifts and their faults for what they are, rather than seeing them as mirror-images of ourselves.

Summary

Having enemies and being prejudiced are often defence mechanisms to bolster ourselves when we feel threatened, or when we find it hard to come to terms with what we find unacceptable in ourselves. It is crucial for us then to be honest with ourselves and admit our weakness, our failings or darkness, and then to do something about them. Then we will have a clearer eye to see our neighbours, to distinguish between fact and fantasy, between their individuality and their mass identity (no more 'the Russians', but these Russian human beings), between their virtues and their vices. Once having admitted the evil in ourselves we are more likely to have the humility and insight, as well as the courage, to tackle real external evil more effectively.

6.4. LOVE YOUR ENEMIES

G. K. Chesterton wrote:

> 'The Christian ideal has not been tried and found wanting; it has been found difficult and left untried.'

It is precisely because Jesus' teaching goes to the heart of the matter that we ritualise it, dogmatise it, endlessly debate it—always postponing the day for living it. He preached *metanoia*—that we should change our hearts and minds, the way we look at life. He taught that it is in acknowledging our weakness that we find strength; that we are 'blessed' if we hunger and thirst for righteousness, and if we are peacemakers; that we can rely on the unconditional love of a God whom we may call 'Abba'; that the offer of this relationship is open to *all* people, and hence no one is excluded unless they choose to be. He taught us to examine our own hearts: no one is without sin, as he showed those who accused the woman caught in adultery. He taught us that we should pay attention to the beam in our own eye, and less to the speck in somebody else's.

For Jesus there was no distinction between religion, culture and politics, and he would find the divisions we make false and unreal. He would agree with Gandhi, who said that those who claim religion has nothing to do with politics (not party politics) do not understand what religion is about. Jesus saw life as a whole, human and divine, with active love as the key to relationships:

Love God
Love your neighbour
Love yourself
Love your enemy

Jesus, when questioned, said that there are two commandments upon which all the law and the prophets depend, and that there is no other command greater than these:

Love God with your entire self, and
Love your neighbour as yourself
(Mark 12: 28 – 34)

The first of these echoes the hauntingly beautiful words of Deuteronomy 6.5—words to be written in our hearts, and taught to our children. The second commandment is ancient too, and echoes Leviticus 19: 18; but note that this is a dramatic double commandment. Jesus assumed as axiomatic that we love ourselves, and then said: as you love yourself, in the same way love your neighbour.

Jesus takes this further in his Sermon on the Mount: 'You have learned that they were told, "Love your neighbour, hate your enemy". But what I tell you is this: Love your enemies and pray for your persecutors' (Matt.5: 43 – 45). This is the way God acts. As there is no place or person foreign to the love of God, so too must there be no place or person foreign to our love. What is this—unpractical idealism, or radical pragmatism uncovering at once both the source of the problems and their solution? This is hard, risky, makes us vulnerable, and is foolish. It is so dramatic that we must *do* it, or walk no more with Jesus.

Jesus knew that his vision was possible, but that the reality was very different. There would need to be a growth towards the realisation of the

Kingdom. So he enjoined us to seek reconciliation every time our relationships break, by giving and receiving forgiveness. Because life is continuous, and growth towards the Kingdom is dynamic, forgiveness is never once-for-all but is also continuous—it must be renewed, as he put it, 'until seventy times seven'.

For discussion:

Consider the following examples:

1. The caste system in India earlier this century excluded millions of Hindus from social, cultural, political and religious life. So severe was the plight of these 'untouchables' that in some states they were not allowed near the temples, lest their shadow defile the holy place. To begin to break this way of perceiving and treating them, Mahatma Gandhi adopted an 'untouchable' child into his family and called the 'untouchables' *Harijans* which means 'children of God', urging all Indians to use the same word. He said that either they would reject him, or else the new word would become so powerful that they would have to change their way of thinking, and hence their ways of behaving.
2. When Willi Brandt was the West German Chancellor, he made a visit to Poland in December 1970, and went to the Warsaw Ghetto. He went in a spirit of penance, seeking forgiveness for the German people—in effect, asking for love from former enemies, and offering in return the hand of friendship.
3. At a time when political relations between Egypt and the modern state of Israel had apparently reached total stalemate, the President of Egypt, Anwar Sadat, took a significant risk. In November 1977, he flew to Israel, and went to the Knesset (parliament) in Jerusalem to seek peace with his country's 'enemies'. In the relations between Israeli and Arab, this move was unprecedented.
4. The Lancaster House Agreement created the independent country of Zimbabwe, after the bitter guerrilla war in the former British colony of Rhodesia. The first elections in the new Zimbabwe returned Robert Mugabe as Prime Minister—a man who had been a guerrilla leader for many years, and had been jailed by the Smith regime. In his independence speech, in April 1980, he called upon all Zimbabweans, black and white, to forgive their former enemies and work together to build a new Zimbabwe.

Do you consider these to be real examples of 'loving enemies', or of a 'change of heart'? If so, why do you think this is the case? If not, what do you think the motivations were? And also, in the light of subsequent events, have the initiatives been neutralised? If so, how could they be revitalised?

Do you think that 'loving our enemies' is a *practical* possibility in the current world situation?

6.5. CONVERTING THE IMAGINATION

Left to ourselves, the fragmentation, the woundedness, hurt, anger and isolation in us are simply felt as a lack: we don't have the equipment we need to cope with what lies ahead. But in the life of grace, our inner mess and dividedness can be seen as something else—as a sign of the exploring urge, the creative unrest in us. We are not *finished* beings, for what would be the point of life in a world of time and change if we were? Growing, *becoming* a self, is at every point a process vulnerable to damage, frustration and distortion. It is not that we are robbed of our deepest possibilities; we have yet to discover them.

Mature self-awareness depends very largely on grasping the fact that we are *in* the world of time, change and chance. We *can't* start with a clean slate. As soon as an individual is here in the world, he or she at once begins to receive impressions, to be formed in this way or that. There is not much point in resenting this, since we don't in fact control the processes of the world. We need somehow to come to the point where past frustration, failure or injury are accepted as part of the world that is 'given' to us, the total context we're in; and then they become the material we have to make sense of, the raw material of 'spiritual' life. By that we mean simply a human life committed to understanding and transforming its environment—a life that's active, rather than passive, re-active or resentful.

So the emptiness or poverty in us is our *incompleteness*, the fact that we have yet to finish our story and make something of our world (including our own memories). Realising this is a 'conversion' because it means seeing the world as carrying a kind of invitation to thought and action, and so a stimulus to further growth: a gift, not a threat; an opportunity.

It means that we can look at our memories not as a simple record of things done by us and to us, fixed and final, but as a set of data we constantly have to rethink and from which we constantly learn more. We are not doomed or trapped by the past; it is a source of insight, for understanding how we and other people interact now. And we can look at the uncertain future not as a threat we have to try and master by strengthening our defences, but as a realm of surprising opportunities that we could never have created for ourselves: a time of grace.

If this begins to happen, then our imagination is no longer imprisoned by fantasy—by projecting hostility on to the world around us. Imagination, working properly, ought to be taking us deeper *into* the reality of things and people, not covering up this reality. Imagination can and should be a dimension of love: holding something or someone in our attention, thinking our way inside them, seeing the world from another standpoint—which can only occur if we believe that our incompleteness can be enriched by sharing another perspective, that we can *never* say, 'I've understood as much as I intend to understand, and I'm stopping here'. (Much of the first chapter of *Beginning Now, Part 2—Peacemaking in Practice* is concerned with precisely this question. It offers practical suggestions for beginning to 'convert our imagination'.)

We must stress at this point that we don't believe the world's problems are instantly solved by 'converted imagination'. We don't believe that attention and understanding will disarm the Soviet Union, and we certainly don't believe that attention and understanding should lead us to underestimate the hurtful intentions of an enemy. But faced with the current deadlock in international relations, it seems reasonable enough to ask whether we can ever find a language to speak to each other, which will somehow communicate an awareness of the other's fear and sense of poverty, a language of solidarity rather than of judgement. A first step, of course, is finding the words for our own fear and poverty. Admissions of weakness or uncertainty, admission that we do not have a monopoly on righteousness, are not politically popular. However, it is not the job of the Church to be politically popular. The Church must hold up a vision of a world committed to love and understanding, based on a candid acceptance of our own individual and collective weakness.

This is a hard road to tread, and without the inner discipline of prayer, discussed in Chapter 4, we will not be able to sustain this vision, nor find a language in which to express it.

* * * * *

We have assumed all the way through that our reflections on peace and peacemaking as Christians must come back to the sense that we do not live from our own power, resource or initiative. Healthy human community doesn't 'just happen' as a result of various historical accidents, or as a straightforward natural fact. The knots of hostility are only fully untied when we are enabled to see that we are, in creation, covenant, and church, *called* to community and *trusted* to make sense and beauty of the world. The hope of creative and balanced life together rests not on a blandly cheerful view of what sort of beings we are, but on a belief in the stability and resourcefulness of God as a presence from which no violence or failure can ever cut us off. The danger is not that God will wash his hands of us, but that we will keep him as an 'enemy' and make ourselves incapable of seeing that creation is the work of faithful love. The risks of the present world situation are enormous: but for the believer, the risk of a nuclear holocaust is frightening not so much because it threatens our death (we ought to be able to cope with that) as because of *what it would show the human race to have become*—'without hope and without God'.

God would not have deserted us; but we should have behaved as if we had never heard the promise of the Kingdom, and Jesus had lived and died for nothing. 'It's not death I fear', said a friend once, 'it's the death of love'.

If you fear that too, perhaps it's time to look again at what the gospel sets you free to do—beginning now.

Beginning Now—Order Form

Beginning Now materials available are:

Item A: *Part 1, Peacemaking Theology—a study book for individuals and groups*
Item B: *Part 2, Peacemaking in Practice—a handbook for individuals, families and small groups*
Item C: Cassette tape for group leaders and others—suggested ways of using the material in both books

To: Dunamis, St James's Church,
197 Piccadilly, London W1V 9LF

Please send me:

____	copies of item A @ £2.00 each	________
____	copies of item B @ £2.00 each	________
____	copies of item C @ £1.50 each	________
____	packs of A+B+C @ £5.00 each	________
____	packs of 6 of A @ £10.50 each	________
____	packs of 6 of B @ £10.50 each	________
____	group leader's packs* @ £21.50 each	________

*Six of A+six of B+C

Goods total	________
Add postage and packing 20%	________
TOTAL	________

I enclose cheque/postal order for __________ (cheques payable to: St James's Church, Dunamis Project)

Name ____

Address ____

____

Phone ____

Please print